MW01627495

APHRODISIACS

with a twist

by Mark Sexauer

Photography by Charity Burggraaf
Food styling by Kimberly Swedelius
Design by Stephanie Hansen
Production management by Elizabeth Cromwell/Books in Flight

ISBN 978-0-615-68356-0

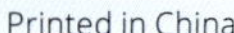

Printed in China

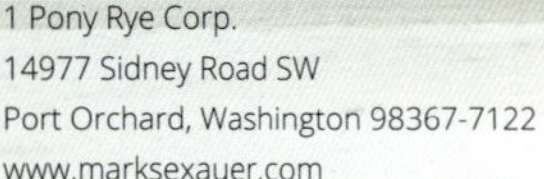

1 Pony Rye Corp.
14977 Sidney Road SW
Port Orchard, Washington 98367-7122
www.marksexauer.com

Thank-yous to people not directly involved but who helped make this a reality one way or another, in no particular order:

Christine Stahl and Robert Sexauer

My immediate and extended family

The Paron Family

Henry

Kristin Mills and Ardie Sameti

Kate Basart

Kelli Adams-Carson

Campari USA

House Spirits

Eric Fahsel

The Washington State chapter of The United States Bartenders Guild and the Eastside Bartenders Association. The Seattle area has one of the best collections of talent in this industry, period.

All drink recipes by Mark Sexauer except: Page 59, with permission.

To my daughter, Isabella.
Throughout my life of regrets, mistakes, stumbles, falls—and worse—you are the guiding light that keeps me going, and with a damn smile the whole time!

Table of Contents

Aphro-what?

Throughout history and in almost every culture, human beings have been looking for ways to elicit and heighten the sexual experience. There were no food scientists or health codes a thousand years ago, and explanations of certain foods were left open for varying interpretation.

According to the *Oxford English Dictionary,* the word "aphrodisiac" first appears in the early 1700s. Originating from Greek mythology, Aphrodite was the goddess of beauty, fertility, and sexual love.

No scientific evidence has proven that any specific food has direct effect on sexual function, but a good number of foods have a long-standing history as suspected sexual stimulants. What better way to explore using these historical aphrodisiacs than by mixing them with alcohol and making cocktails?

Isn't alcohol an aphrodisiac already?

An aphrodisiac is a substance that directly triggers your sexual desire. It could be a shape, smell, or sensation. Alcohol is a very powerful substance, but does not move the dial on your sex drive.

Alcohol tends to disinhibit more than anything else. Imbibers of alcohol can be less shy and more open to experimenting as well as communicating. Some studies have shown that small amounts of alcohol can raise your libido, but in high quantities it can have the opposite effect. Your lowered inhibitions aren't really turning you on, they just make you more likely to do things you wouldn't normally do, which includes nonsexual things. How many people have ever thought it was a great idea to speed down a steep street in a shopping cart while drunk?

Alcohol can also dehydrate your body, decreasing lubrication in women and making it harder for men to perform.

Responsibility

I shouldn't have to explain the dangers of drinking and driving. If you drink, don't drive, and if you drive, don't drink. Enjoying alcohol responsibly makes for a fantastically more enjoyable evening.

Technique

First, don't be scared or intimidated at all! Start by going to a good bar in your area. Watch the bartender and don't worry so much about style or technique. Just watch them. How are they shaking and what are they using to shake? After seeing the process of pouring ingredients and mixing a cocktail, you will feel much more comfortable doing it at home. I have some pointers on everything from the ice you use to equipment and glassware, so do a little reading and a little barhopping. Once you have everything together, just go for it and have fun. Fun and a little humor is part of the cocktail culture! Don't take yourself too seriously and you will already be on your way to becoming a good bartender.

There are hundreds of books about how to bartend, and I won't take up precious recipe space getting too deep into it, but if you are a novice then there are some basics that you should know.

Using This Book

This book is designed to provide drinks for entertainment at parties, a fun, intimate night with your partner, or professional bartenders looking for new inspiration. Some of the recipes are intricate and involve making ingredients and syrups ahead of time, while others are easy and straightforward. Of course, the best aphrodisiac is a healthy relationship. The whole idea of the book—no matter your situation—is to have fun.

A note on vodka

Vodka has a long and rich history and is also the country's most popular spirit, so you will see a number of vodka-based cocktails throughout this book. If you have not tried one of the many well-made spirits as a base ingredient, then some of these recipes will be a great opportunity to branch out and stumble onto something you might love.

I typically do not turn to vodka when mixing drinks because it is a neutral grain spirit. The majority of brands have alcohol content but almost no flavor profile. For this reason, when creating well-made cocktails, a lot of bartenders shy away from using vodka—at least as a base ingredient.

Poor results

The drinks featured in each photograph were made to recipe. If your cocktail doesn't look exactly like the one pictured, don't worry about it! Seasonal changes and variations in ingredients can affect certain products, which in turn change their weight or color. Start by making simpler drinks with ingredients you recognize. If you are making a drink and it doesn't meet your expectations, try again or move on to another one. Each person's palate is different, and although your friends may love it, you may not—that's the nature of food! Some of the drinks in this book have very strong and distinct flavor profiles geared to certain palates, while others are very mild and friendly.

Ingredients

Everything you use in a drink is important in some way. Would you use cheese from a can when the recipe asks for smoked gouda? Of course not! Use high-quality ingredients for high-quality results. Always lean toward fresh squeezed juices whenever possible.

This doesn't mean that you have to go out and buy an expensive juicer. Cheesecloth is an inexpensive alternative and can juice almost everything just as well. Even a reamer does an amazing job of juicing citrus. Make an effort to use fresh squeezed juices if a recipe calls for it. Alternatives to fresh juice will dramatically change the flavor profile. Don't believe me? Go taste the difference between canned and freshly squeezed pineapple juice.

Shaken not stirred

For the most part, the recipes in this book use some sort of fruit, vegetable, or other edible plant life, and a lot of the drinks demand a good shake. Shaking a cocktail is much more than shaking with ice. I've seen a number of "professional" bartenders give a couple limp shakes and strain the drink into a glass. Water is a very important part of nearly every cocktail recipe. Without chilling your ingredients and the proper amount of cold water, a good drink will be mediocre.

Stirring is essential to drinks like the Manhattan. If there are only spirits in the recipe (including vermouths and some liqueurs), the general rule is it must be stirred. Stirring will give you cold and clear results as well as a little less dilution. Shaking introduces lots of air and bubbles into a drink, giving a Martini or Manhattan a cloudy look. Shaking is utilized in drinks that contain juice or a purée.

When shaking, do so for at least 10 to 20 seconds—much more if there is a whole egg or egg white. Your hands should be cold and your arms should hurt; those are signs that a successful shaking took place.

Muddling

Muddling is an important skill to squeeze out juices and essential oils and is a great technique for incorporating flavors. There is rarely a need to muddle with ice. It creates more work for yourself and in many cases is counterproductive. Another tip worth mentioning is to use a metal, tin, or very thick tempered glass. Many a bartender has scars from shattered glass. Muddle ingredients with heavy pressure and a twisting motion to get the desired effect.

When looking to purchase a muddler, stay away from cheap ones with stained wood that can chip away into your drinks.

The Right Equipment

Mixing drinks at home is easy and can be done at very little cost. If this is your first stab at making cocktails, prepare to fall in love with the cocktail culture!

The cocktails in this book are based on professional bartending as we know it today. If you happen to be a seasoned home or professional bartender, most of this equipment is well known to you. Like any good chef or carpenter who takes pride in what they do, you must have the right tools. The following is a list of basic bartending equipment you will see behind modern bars and used throughout this book.

Bar spoon

The spoon typically holds an eighth of an ounce. Look for a spoon with a nice balanced weight; try to stay away from cheap versions with red plastic muddling tips.

Shaker

To start out, try a restaurant supply store or shop online for an all-in-one shaker (called a cobbler shaker). Look for something to combine ingredients, shake with ice, and strain easily. I've even used a Mason jar in a pinch!

Strainer

You will use a simple hawthorn strainer a thousand times. Shopping online or at a restaurant supply store will be your best bet. Look for a strainer with tight coils to help catch various food bits and larger chunks of ice. Another frequently used item is a fine strainer, used to double strain (after using a hawthorn strainer, pour into a fine strainer to remove seeds and fruit bits). Any small, fine strainer will work.

Juicer

I like to use a tabletop juicer when making larger batches of juice for a party or busy night at the bar. Some bartenders use a hand press. In a pinch there is also the inexpensive reamer. The best cocktails use the best ingredients; fresh juice should be a priority for all drinks you consume. However you juice fruits and vegetables doesn't really matter as long as you are using fresh ingredients.

Jigger

Jiggers are an essential part of a bartender's tool kit. A good bartender can measure by sight, but there are numerous drinks (depending on the spirit or liqueur) that can be completely thrown off by just a couple of drops. Get into the habit of measuring everything. Consistency is very important when guests are paying $10 to $20 for cocktails. You must deliver a well-made, balanced, and measured drink every time.

Containers

I like to frequent secondhand shops and garage sales to find unique container choices. Use whatever is convenient for you to store and pour your homemade syrups and juices: small pitchers, squeeze bottles, cups, or even wine bottles with the labels washed off.

Muddler

There are many different sizes and styles of muddlers on the market, and any will work. I've already mentioned this, but it's worth repeating: stay away from cheap muddlers with a stain or paint on the outside. After time, the stain chips away into the drink. We will be using a muddler on and off throughout this book to extract oils and juices from various fruits and vegetables. Look for a basic lathed, bare wood muddler, which can be treated with food-safe mineral oil.

Knife

There are very few rules for choosing your knives. There is only one important rule with knives that must always be followed: make sure they are sharp—very sharp. Some bartenders like a large chef's knife or bread knife for cutting through fruit and tough skins. Others prefer the smaller paring knife, which is great for cutting small garnishes and most small fruits. Sharpen your knives at least twice a year. Always use a cutting board, and for the love, curl your fingers in when holding and cutting!

Soda siphon

Soda siphons are used in a number of recipes in this book and come in handy quite often. Make sure to get plenty of CO_2 cartridges with your siphon. These are used to make soda water, homemade syrups, sodas, and even whole cocktails.

Cream whipper

In this book there are a couple of flavored foam and homemade whipped cream recipes that call for a cream whipper. You can make whipped cream with a whisk or electric mixer, but I prefer a cream whipper for its versatility. I like the one made by iSi, which comes in a 1 pint or 1 quart size. Don't forget the box of N_2O cartridges!

Other Tools

There are many more bar tools in addition to those listed above; this is simply a general list to get you started with mixing drinks. Some recipes will use standard kitchen equipment such as a food processor, pots, pans, and large bowls for mixing and serving. If you don't have any of the equipment used in a particular recipe, just move on to another, or use this book as a reason to purchase that piece of kitchen equipment you have always wanted!

Stocking Your Bar

Now that we've gone through the basic tools you need to put on a good show, it's time to go over what to pour. Product knowledge in this industry is very important and can seem overwhelming. It takes many years to become competent in even the most basic of bar stock. No matter where you stand on the liquor knowledge ladder, take your time and have fun reading about the different products and spirits. I recommend picking one or two recipes at a time and purchasing only the bottles you need. Eventually you will want your liquor cabinet to start resembling this minimalist list.

One bottle of each of the following

* Vodka
* Triple sec or orange liqueur
* Gin
* Sweet vermouth
* Dry vermouth—Vermouth is wine based and needs to be refrigerated, as its quality can start to diminish after a month or so.
* Whiskey—scotch/bourbon/rye/Irish
* Rum
* Tequila—100% agave
* Bottle of bitters—like Angostura

Small cans or bottles of the following

* Cranberry juice
* Tonic water
* Soda water
* Cola

Continued...

* Diet cola
* Lemon-lime soda

The majority of spirits cost between $20 to $50 for one bottle. Bars and restaurants spend a small fortune on their initial liquor orders. Take your time and search out bargains; most brands also offer much cheaper 350-milliliter bottles, perfect for the home bartender.

Have a party

I've heard of a number of people who have hosted a "stock my bar" party. The idea is to call up as many friends as you can and have them each bring one bottle of liquor. Minimize doubles by assigning spirit categories. For example, "Bob, bring a gin. Jill, you bring a rum." Provide food and drinks and you'll see how quickly your bar stock builds up. If you get eight people to come, you've got everything on the minimalist list.

Glassware

Glassware is much more important than some people think. Your wine glass is not just a vessel to get wine from a bottle into your mouth. The shape and design of glassware continues to evolve along with beer, wine, and spirits. A champagne glass, for example, is typically slender with a long stem. The stem prevents your hand from warming the champagne and keeps fingerprints off the glass. The glass is long and narrow, so visually the bubbles must travel farther. Every aspect, from the diameter of the bowl opening to glass thickness, is taken into account.

Glassware has been categorized by its specific purpose. Have you ever had a good red wine out of a paper cup? Try it, and you'll see that the same wine tastes much better in a large red wine glass! Your hand does not warm the wine, and the glass closes slightly at the top, targeting the complex smells of the wine to your nose when you take a sip.

Try to use glassware similar to that in the photographs; it will help make the drink the best it can be.

I've mentioned this already, but I really like going to secondhand shops and garage sales to find unique and older-style glassware. Although some large retail stores will carry great glassware, you'll be surprised how useful your grandma's cabinet is when you start snooping around.

The most popular glassware

* Cocktail (or martini)—*4 to 8 ounces*
* Collins (or chimney)—*10 to 14 ounces*
* Lowball (old-fashioned or rocks)—*6 to 10 ounces*
* Highball (or double old-fashioned)—*12 to 16 ounces*
* Coupe (champagne saucer)—*5 to 8 ounces*
* Champagne flute—*6 to 10 ounces*
* Snifter—*16 to 24 ounces (with a typical pour being 2 ounces at a time)*
* Red wine glass—*8 to 22 ounces (with a typical restaurant pour being 5 to 6 ounces)*
* White wine glass—*8 to 16 ounces (with a typical restaurant pour being 5 to 6 ounces)*
* Shot glass—*up to 4 ounces*

Simple Syrups

Simple syrups are used in every bar and are a powerful tool. We will be using simple syrups throughout this book, and there are a number of techniques to use depending on the ingredient and type of drink. The base recipe for simple syrup is so easy; it's amazing some companies make money selling it.

Typically, bars use a 1:1 ratio of sugar to water. You can lower the sweetness level by doing a 1:2 ratio of sugar to water, or raise it by using the common 2:1, creating less "filler" volume in a cocktail—even 3:1 ratios are somewhat common. Either way, there is no reason to buy simple syrup. It is way too easy to make, and the store-bought brands can have high-fructose corn syrup and other artificial ingredients and preservatives.

Variations on simple syrups include substituting different kinds of exotic and not-so-exotic sugars such as honey, brown sugar, turbinado, agave, Barbados, even calorie-free alternatives. The list goes on! Possibilities are vast, with bartenders around the world creating syrups with many complex and hard-to-find ingredients. How about a lavender syrup—black pepper, eucalyptus, or blue violet agave? Whether a novice or a professional bartender, simple and flavored syrups are a useful tool with which to experiment.

Make sure to sterilize your choice of container. I like to fill a container with boiling water and then pour it out to dry. Just a little bacteria will send all your hard work downhill quickly, and with a stomachache to boot! Most bacteria we would be concerned with die at around 165°F. So boiling water—which of course is around 212°F—does the trick. Another method is to rest your glass jars or containers in the oven at 250°F for a couple of minutes. At this heat your containers will be sterile. Don't put your rubber tops in there though! Use a little common sense and don't subject your glass to cold water after heating.

Simple Syrup

All recipes in this book use a 1:1 ratio of sugar to water unless otherwise noted.

1 cup water
1 cup sugar

Heat water in a saucepan over medium-high heat and add sugar. Stir until completely dissolved and let cool. Store in the refrigerator for up to 1 month.

[Variations]

Raw Sugar Simple Syrup
Use 1 cup Sugar in the Raw instead of sugar.

Agave Simple Syrup
Use 1 cup agave nectar instead of sugar.

Honey Simple Syrup
Use 1 cup honey instead of sugar.

Strawberry Simple Syrup

Another way simple syrups can be used is to extract or infuse flavor into them. The strawberries can of course be substituted with any fruit, vegetable, herb, or spice. Most of the recipes in the book using simple syrups will use this method as well as heating the water with herbs or spices to infuse them all together.

1 cup (or so) strawberries, hulled and diced
1 cup Simple Syrup (see above)
1 ounce 80-proof vodka

Continued...

Place strawberries in a bowl and cover with simple syrup. With a muddler (or anything) lightly press on some of the strawberries to release just a little of the juice into the simple syrup. Cover with plastic wrap and refrigerate overnight. The next day, strain without crushing into your choice of container and add the vodka to act as a preservative. Bottle and use for 1 month.

Homemade Grenadine

Grenadine is essentially pomegranate simple syrup. Pomegranate molasses and orange blossom water are very commonly used by bartenders to add complexity. Some store-bought grenadines tend to be cherry flavored so it can seem a little confusing. Read the ingredient list on a store-bought grenadine bottle and you will understand why I would never use it.

- 1 cup 100% pomegranate juice
- 1 cup superfine sugar
- 1 tablespoon fresh lemon juice
- 1 tablespoon pomegranate molasses
- 1 teaspoon orange blossom water
- 1 ounce vodka (to help preserve)

Combine all ingredients in a Mason jar with a lid and shake it like it owes you money (heat can change the flavor of the delicate pomegranate juice). Add vodka if storing for more than 2 weeks. Taste side by side with the store-bought stuff if you would like to see the massive difference homemade makes.

Garnish Ideas

The cocktails in this book are almost all garnished to some extent or another. Garnishes add a great visual to a drink and show how it was made with care and passion. I've see some garnishes that border on art. Most garnishes are extremely easy to make and take very little prep to get those *ooh* and *aah* reactions. Garnishes can be artsy and showy, but some are truly functional, like squeezing lemon oil on the surface of a martini. You will notice a number of fancy or complicated garnishes throughout the book. There is a lot of information online and in books about advanced garnishing. You can, of course, omit the garnish altogether in most recipes. I recommend just having fun with it! The following is a list of popular drink garnishes:

Twist

Try a Y-peeler for a quick and easy large zest you can twist.

Wedge

Cut a fruit from stem to end and slice into thin or thick wedges.

Wheel

Thin or thick wheels (cross-sectioned slices of fruit) are one of my favorite floating garnishes.

Slice

Also called a half-wheel. Commonly a slit is cut in the middle so the half-wheel can hang on the glass.

Oil

Oils locked in the skin of citrus fruits can be sprayed on top of a drink for show stopping aromatics. Use a vegetable peeler to cut a large thick swath of zest. Hold the zest over a drink and using your finger and thumb, roll it to break open the pores, squeezing oil on the cocktail.

Zest

Cut a thin zest using a zester, or a wide zest using a Y-peeler. The thin zests are usually twisted (a straw to twist it around then slide it off is a good beginner trick) while the wide zests are twisted as well as squeezed.

Fruits

This is a pretty general category but I thought I'd mention it, as in reality this is the most common garnish. Try thinly sliced star fruit, pomegranate seeds, even watermelon balls; just have fun with it!

Flavored sugars

Sugar is used often when rimming a glass. With a food processor, you can easily color and flavor sugar at home. Spread out on a large pan to dry the sugar afterwards.

Chocolate

Shavings tend to melt, which isn't a bad thing. Try a Y-peeler on a chocolate block for sexy chocolate peels.

Candy

I've been served some of the funniest candy garnishes, ranging from penis-shaped lollipops to speared Swedish Fish.

Maraschino cherries

If you must choose store-bought, go to a specialty shop and look for cherries soaking in brandy, or maraschino liqueur—or both. Ordering from a bar supply store will be your best bet. There are also many recipes online. Making your own is easy. Make a point to stay away from the sulfur dioxide, calcium chloride, sugar, FD&C Red 40 food dye, and other things in the modern abomination of maraschino cherries. Yuck.

Grating

Think whole fresh nutmeg grated over eggnog.

Smoking

You can smoke pretty much anything, so be creative! Store-bought smoked salt is an easy alternative.

Drying

You can dry pretty much anything, so only your imagination is the limit! I like dried pineapple strips and dried apple wheels.

Marinated Asparagus

One of many visual aphrodisiacs, the asparagus with its long stem and bulbous head is undeniably reminiscent of manhood. There is literature to suggest that 19th-century grooms were given asparagus on their wedding night to help make the evening a pulse-pounding success. Asparagus is packed with vitamins, potassium, and folic acid. The stalks are high in vitamin E, which aids in many important functions of the body, one of which is helping produce our sexual hormones.

- 2½ pounds fresh asparagus (about 50 stalks, depending on size)
- 2 (1-quart) canning jars
- 1 tablespoon whole black peppercorns
- 1 tablespoon whole yellow mustard seeds
- 1 tablespoon whole coriander seeds
- 1 tablespoon whole allspice berries
- 1 teaspoon dill seed
- 2 tablespoons kosher salt
- 1 cup apple cider vinegar
- 1 cup white wine vinegar
- 2 cups water
- 4 garlic cloves, peeled

Continued...

2 medium jalapeños, cut in half
4 bay leaves

Snap asparagus near the bottom of the stalk. Hold the asparagus up next to the jar and make sure that they are not too tall; if so, snap a little more off the bottom. Bring a large pot of water to a boil. Using tongs, dip each jar into the boiling water for a couple of seconds to sterilize. Using the same water, blanch the asparagus for only about 30 seconds. Using tongs, remove the asparagus and put into an ice bath (large bowl filled with cold water and ice).

While the asparagus is cooling, add all of the dry ingredients to a pot over medium heat. Heat until fragrant; do not burn. Add the vinegars and water and bring to a boil, then remove from heat.

Pack the cooled asparagus into the canning jars with the heads facing up. Push 2 peeled garlic cloves, 2 jalapeño halves, and 2 bay leaves into each jar. Using a ladle, fill each jar with the spice/vinegar mixture, distributing all the spices. You may fill with a little water if needed but leave a ½-inch space in each jar on top. Use a new lid and ring and put into the refrigerator for 48 hours. I let mine sit for longer (at least 4 days) but I understand not being able to wait!

After marinating, use the spears in a Bloody Mary (page 85). There is also a white variety of asparagus that you can use instead of the green. The white works as a great visual contrast to the red tomato juice. Makes two 1-quart jars.

Ice

Ice is extremely important when making a cocktail. It's not only aesthetically interesting, but the goal is to make a cold drink without over-diluting it. Don't use old ice; it may or may not have absorbed the taste of whatever weird stuff is in your freezer.

Make a new batch—or even better—boil some water and make a large ice block. Pour the boiled water into a deep large pan and freeze. You can cut precise pieces to meet your need. A large ice cube will retain its temperature longer than a smaller one. This is hugely beneficial when imbibing pure spirits, such as a bold overproof bourbon.

You can also use large clean ice cube trays—many are available online. You can even get a number of silicone ice molds to add a fun aspect to boring home freezer-ice.

If you'd like, experiment with adding fruit within the ice. I've seen bartenders do pretty fun things like adding toy soldiers or erotic items to ice cubes. This is especially fun for sangria, for which you should always use the largest possible chunk of ice.

You can use a food processor to quickly turn ice into shavings. A canvas bag, called a Lewis Bag, and mallet are commonly used to hand crush large ice cubes into smaller ones, and to finely crush ice. This is also a very fun, active way to crush ice in front of people. This may sound trivial, but only add ice when you are ready to shake the drink. If you add ice before adding additional ingredients, the ice will begin to melt, adding too much water to the recipe.

If anything, I hope you consider what ice you are using, since it is so easy to overlook. Use clean, fresh ice in the shape that will benefit the specific drink you are making. It will only add to your enjoyment, and help you make a better cocktail!

DELUXE

CARROT

Carrots are an incredible resource behind the bar and are surprisingly under used. The imagination is the limit with carrots, whether used as garnishes or as a layer of flavor in the cocktail. Follow these easy recipes as a guideline for utilizing carrots behind the bar.

La Zanahoria

Carrot works hand in hand with caraway-and-anise-drenched aquavit: they were meant for each other. This is a spicy citrusy carroty cocktail that will turn any carrot skeptic into a carrot fan.

1 to 2 thin slices jalapeño (optional)
Small pinch fresh cilantro (optional)
1½ ounces aquavit (I use Krogstad)
¾ ounce carrot juice (if store-bought, make sure it's 100% juice)
½ ounce orange liqueur
½ ounce fresh lime juice
⅓ ounce Simple Syrup (see page 23)

Muddle jalapeños and cilantro in the bottom of a mixing glass, if using. Add remaining ingredients and shake well with ice. Pour all into a Collins glass.

Garnish Idea: Carrot-Salt-Cumin Rim (see below)

[Carrot-Salt-Cumin Rim]

1 tablespoon kosher salt
1 tablespoon minced carrots, dried with a paper towel
1 teaspoon ground cumin
1 lime wedge

Combine salt, carrots, and cumin together on a plate. Use the lime wedge to moisten the rim of the glass, then press glass into the mixture.

Sunset and Sand

Scotch is not reached for as often as other spirits because of its very strong, distinct smoky flavor. Pick a scotch that fits your flavor profile.

1¼ ounces scotch
1 dash smoky scotch, like Laphroaig (optional)
1 ounce fresh orange juice
¾ ounce carrot juice (if store-bought, make sure it's 100% juice)
¾ ounce Cherry Heering
¾ ounce sweet vermouth

Combine all ingredients in a shaker, add ice, and shake hard. Strain into a cocktail glass of choice.

Garnish Idea: Rim glass with Carrot Powder (see below)

[Carrot Powder]

2 medium carrots

Wash and shred carrots and spread around on parchment paper in a large pan. Cook in a preheated 200°F oven for up to 4 hours. Remove from the oven and let cool. Make sure they feel dry and crumble if you crush them with your fingers. For best results use a (very) clean coffee grinder and grind dried shredded carrots until they turn into a kind of dust or powder. Filter through a fine mesh strainer to remove any of the larger bits and store in a sealed container of choice for up to 1 month, refrigerated, as flavor will diminish.

Taproot Sour

A variation of this drink got me to a national spot in a cocktail competition. Surprisingly refreshing, cooking the carrots give them a sweetness that makes this drink like a light carrot dessert.

1½ ounces white rum
1½ ounces Roasted Carrot Juice (see below)
½ ounce fresh lemon juice
1 tablespoon fresh egg white (or more)
Pinch fresh ground allspice (optional)

Combine all ingredients in a shaker, add ice, and shake very hard to emulsify the egg white. Strain or double strain into a cocktail or coupe glass.

Garnish Ideas: Slapped flat-leaf parsley, fresh ground allspice

[Roasted Carrot Juice]

3 medium to large carrots, washed but not peeled
1 tablespoon vegetable oil
2 cups water
¾ cup sugar
¼ teaspoon kosher salt

If the carrots are thick, cut them in half lengthwise; if not, leave whole. Slice the carrots in 1-inch-long slices. Toss together with the vegetable oil and transfer to a sheet pan (use parchment paper if available) and roast in a 400°F oven for about 20 minutes, until tender. Put the roasted carrots in a blender or food processor and add the water. Blend until liquefied. If you're lucky enough to have a Chinoise strainer, use that, or layered cheesecloth works well. Strain out as much liquid as you can; do not push through any carrot purée, just the liquid. Add the sugar and salt, stirring until blended, and pour into a container of choice for up to 1 week, refrigerated. Makes enough for 12 drinks.

STRAWBERRY

Strawberries are one of the most obvious choices of fruit when seduction is the goal for the night. Muddling and juicing are the most common uses for strawberries, but almost any technique will work. They infuse well, although it takes 2 to 3 weeks to achieve the proper flavor.

Elixir of Ezra

If you are unfamiliar with yellow Chartreuse, this drink is a great introduction to it. The complex herbal liqueur has somewhat of a cult following among cocktail enthusiasts. Try it neat and you'll find out why.

1 large ripe strawberry, rinsed and hulled
1½ ounces gin
½ ounce yellow Chartreuse
¼ to ½ ounce orange liqueur (such as Giffard or Cointreau)
1 dash orange bitters

Muddle the strawberry in the bottom of a mixing glass. Add the remaining ingredients and shake hard with ice to break up the strawberry. Double strain into a small cocktail glass of choice.

Garnish Idea: Orange zest, flowered if desired

Fraises Royale

So simple and so easy. It fits as a before-dinner drink as well as dessert. By the fire or a summertime sunset, sometimes it really is the simple things.

Champagne or sparkling wine, to fill
1 ounce Strawberry Purée (see below), or to taste

Pour sparkling wine about halfway up the glass. Slowly pour or spoon in Strawberry Purée and slowly stir to incorporate. Fill the rest of the glass up with champagne or sparkling wine very slowly to avoid a spillover. Make sure to tip the glass as vertically as possible when pouring to cut down on agitation.

Garnish Ideas: Mint leaf, floating thin strawberry slice

[Strawberry Purée]

1 cup ripe strawberries, diced
¼ cup water

Combine strawberries and water in a blender or food processor and blend until liquid. Strain out seeds.

Give In to Temptation

Chocolaty and strong, so be very careful, this one goes down fast. Very fast.

1½ ounces vodka (also try vanilla vodka, preferably homemade)
1½ ounces Chocolate Liqueur (see below)
Strawberry Foam (see below), to top

Combine vodka and Chocolate Liqueur in a mixing glass and add ice. Shake hard and strain into a cocktail glass. Top with Strawberry Foam.

Garnish Ideas: Chocolate shavings, strawberry slice

[Chocolate Liqueur]

Almost all store-bought syrup has high-fructose corn syrup. This recipe uses real chocolate (cacao) to create a syrup perfect for hundreds of uses. I'm sure you can think of some.

2 cups water
1 cup sugar
⅓ cup unsweetened cocoa powder
1 cup grain vodka

Combine the water, sugar, and cocoa powder in a pot over medium-high heat. Stir until uniform and smooth. Remove from heat and add the vodka. Pour into a squeezable container and keep, refrigerated, for up to 2 weeks.

[Strawberry Foam]

Can be used for more than just topping cocktails . . .

6 ounces sugar
6 ounces water
2 teaspoons powdered gelatin

6 ounces fresh lemon juice

6 ounces Strawberry Purée (see page 45)

4 egg whites

In a medium pot, add the sugar, water, and gelatin. Heat over medium, stirring constantly with a whisk until gelatin is mostly dissolved, then remove from heat. The mixture should not come to a boil. Add lemon juice and Strawberry Purée, and let the mixture sit until cool, at least 15 to 20 minutes. Finely strain mixture (to remove pulp) into pourable container and add the egg whites, mixing briefly to incorporate. Pour mixture into a 1-quart iSi whip canister and charge with 2 cream (N_2O) cartridges. Refrigerate for 4 to 6 hours to cool completely. Shake before using.

Never Say Never

The base of the Never Say Never is a daiquiri formula, but with the added herbs and our sultry strawberry, we have a deliciously balanced cocktail. Make sure to slap the basil leaf; it opens up the pores and helps release its aroma.

1 large ripe strawberry, rinsed and hulled
2 medium-sized basil leaves
2 to 4 mint leaves
2 ounces white rum
1 ounce fresh lime juice
¾ ounce Simple Syrup (see page 23)

Combine the strawberry, basil, and mint together in a mixing glass. Muddle to break up strawberry and bruise herbs. Add ice and remaining ingredients, shake hard, and double strain into a cocktail glass of choice.

Garnish Idea: Slapped basil leaf float

Northern Snow

The condensed milk gives this drink a creamy but not too rich flavor. The walnut liqueur is fun, but the much more common amaretto works well also. If you don't want to wait for homemade strawberry vodka, store-bought will do.

2 ounces Strawberry Vodka (see below)
2 ounces Strawberry Purée (see page 45)
¼ ounce walnut liqueur (or amaretto)
2 tablespoons sweetened condensed milk

Combine ingredients in a mixing glass, add ice, and shake hard to emulsify the condensed milk and incorporate flavor. Pour into a double old-fashioned glass.

Garnish Idea: Shaved chocolate

[Strawberry Vodka]

Tastes amazing served neat or chilled as well.

2 pints (about 1¼ pounds) ripe strawberries, hulled and diced
1 (750-milliliter) bottle grain vodka

Place strawberries into a sealable container. Add vodka and cover. Store in a dark place where you are apt to see it and shake it once a day for 7 to 21 days, depending on the flavor you would like. Taste daily after 7 days. Once ready, finely strain and store in a bottle of choice. Will hold for about 2 months before starting to lose flavor.

Starry Night

Wine in cocktails is very versatile and common (think sangria). Feel free to play with the amount of balsamic, as products and palates vary so much. Remember, you can always add but it's harder to take away.

1½ ounces brandy (bourbon also works well)
½ ounce Cabernet Sauvignon (preferably a cheaper one with high residual sugar)
½ ounce Strawberry-Pepper-Balsamic Syrup (see below)
2 dashes Angostura bitters

Combine ingredients in a mixing glass with ice and shake hard. Strain or double strain into a cocktail glass of choice.

Garnish Ideas: Floating thin strawberry slice, crushed pepper

[Strawberry-Pepper-Balsamic Syrup]

1 cup aged balsamic vinegar
½ cup sugar
4 ripe strawberries, rinsed, hulled, and quartered
5 whole peppercorns

Combine all ingredients in a medium pot over medium-high heat. Bring to a boil, then reduce heat to medium-low. Cook uncovered to reduce for about 30 minutes, until it sticks like a thick syrup to a spoon. Remove from heat and strain out solids. Pour syrup into a container of choice (it will continue to thicken). Keep, refrigerated, for up to 1 week.

MINT

Most people automatically think of the classic mojito or mint julep when they think of mint in cocktails. Its aromatics blend extremely well with many ingredients like lime, most spirits, and even chocolate. Pick off a mint leaf and smell it. Now put one in the palm of your hand, give it nice firm smack, and then take another whiff. The difference is amazing. Just a little bruising is all you need to release the wonderfully potent mint flavor and aroma. You have many options when using mint in your creations: everything from spearmint and peppermint to chocolate mint and pineapple mint.

Overgrown Meadow

The mojito is an obvious mint cocktail and is almost always bastardized, at least whenever I order one. The mint flavor isn't there, the rum is low quality, the juices are almost never fresh. Nothing ruins a mojito like opening a can of mojito mix! I like to deconstruct it a little and really blast your mouth with flavor. This doesn't look like a mojito but it has all the elements and taste of what the minty, herbal, citrusy, and alcoholic concoction should be.

8 mint sprigs
2 ounces white rum
1 ounce fresh lime juice
1 ounce Simple Syrup (see page 23)
Sparkling water, to taste

Muddle mint in the bottom of a mixing glass. Normally you just want to bruise the mint, sometimes even just slap it, but in this case we are tearing the stuff up. Muddle hard. Add rum, lime juice, and simple syrup, and shake extremely hard with ice to really break apart the mint. Strain into a cocktail glass and add a little sparkling water to taste. I like about ½ ounce for just a little effervescence.

Garnish Ideas: Lime wheel float, mint leaf

Mint Julep

The focus of this book is on original recipes. There are hundreds, if not thousands of books dedicated to classic cocktail recipes, but the mint julep is a weakness of mine. Not only has it been woven into our culture through time, but the simple straightforward approach is a perfect way to enjoy bourbon and mint together in a flavor harmony that I have yet to find in another cocktail. This is based on David Woodrich's take on the classic.

16 mint sprigs, divided
¼ teaspoon powdered sugar
1 ounce spring water
1 teaspoon sugar
3 ounces Kentucky bourbon

Put 10 mint sprigs in the bottom of a mixing glass. Add powdered sugar and spring water and muddle. Do not destroy the mint, just crush to release the oils and a fragrance. Once muddled, let sit for 10 minutes. Yes, 10 minutes; this helps enhance the mint flavor. Strain the mint-infused water into a pre-chilled, preferably silver, cup, but a double old-fashioned glass works fine. Put 6 mint leaves in the bottom of the glass, add sugar, and muddle. Again, do not destroy the mint, just macerate. Fill the glass with crushed ice, packing it down as you add more ice. Add the bourbon and stir until frost appears on the outside of the glass. Top with more crushed ice.

Garnish Ideas: Large fresh mint sprig, sprinkled powdered sugar

Una Taza

Pimm's No. 1 is making a comeback. Not a huge one, but the Pimm's Cup is still a blip on the radar after over a hundred years of being made. A recent episode of a popular TV show about Prohibition has sparked some renewed interest. This pisco version has a plum flavor quality to it, nice for summer sipping.

2 slices English cucumber (poker chip–sized)
10 large mint leaves
¾ ounce pisco
1 ounce Pimm's No. 1
½ ounce fresh lime juice
½ ounce Simple Syrup (see page 23)
2 dashes Angostura bitters
2 ounces Sexauer's Ginger Beer (see page 157) or store-bought

Muddle cucumber and mint in the bottom of a mixing glass. Add remaining ingredients except the ginger beer and shake lightly with ice only to incorporate ingredients. Pour into a pint or Collins glass and top with ginger beer.

Garnish Idea: Large mint sprig

CHILE

Chile spice/heat is hard to work with in cocktails, same as food. You don't want too much heat as it takes away from flavor and stops being enjoyable. Everything is up to personal taste, but I strive for the drink to just have a hint of chile heat on the back end. People have different tolerances with heat but remember: you can almost always add, but you can't take away. A common misconception with chiles is that the heat is in the seeds. This is not true; the heat is concentrated in the interior veins near the seed heart. The seeds have more heat than say, the skin, but only because of the close contact with the veins.

Chipotle Fresca

Chipotles are smoke-dried chiles and have a very strong, unique flavor to them. This drink will pique the interest of those whose palates enjoy scotch.

1½ ounces gin
½ ounce fresh lemon juice
¾ ounce Chipotle Agave Syrup (see below)
Sparkling wine, to top

Combine the gin, lemon juice, and Chipotle Agave Syrup in a mixing glass and add ice. Shake hard and strain or double strain into a cocktail glass of choice. Top with sparkling wine.

Garnish Idea: Lemon twist

[Chipotle Agave Syrup]

1 cup water
1 cup Agave nectar
6 good-sized dried chipotle chiles

Combine the water and agave nectar in a medium pot over medium heat. Stir until a uniform syrup is created. Drop in chiles, cover, and bring to a simmer. Simmer for 30 minutes, then remove from heat. Let cool to room temperature. Strain out the chiles, pressing on them to release flavor. An overnight in the refrigerator helps to infuse the flavors. Store the syrup in a container of choice for up to 1 month, refrigerated.

Sadie's Cousin

Rum and pineapple will always have an affinity for each other. The chile pepper is a natural addition to this well-rounded drink.

2 to 4 thin jalapeño slices
4 pineapple chunks (grape-sized)
2 ounces gold rum
½ ounce Lillet Blanc
½ ounce fresh lemon juice
½ ounce Agave Simple Syrup (see page 23)

Muddle the jalapeño and pineapple in the bottom of a mixing glass to release juice and oils. Add the remaining ingredients and ice. Shake hard and double strain into a cocktail glass.

Garnish Idea: Large, thin, diagonally cut jalapeño

Sangrita

A traditional sipper to tequila, think of sangrita as a sort of palate cleanser. Typically enjoyed with blanco and reposado tequilas. Take a sip of tequila, then a sip of sangrita. Repeat until both are gone. When purchasing tequila, make sure you see "100% agave" on the label. By the way, the Americanized version makes a great marinade and egg topper.

[Americanized Sangrita]

1½ cups fresh tomato juice (canned will work)
¾ cup fresh orange juice
3 ounces fresh lime juice
2 tablespoons agave nectar
1 tablespoon hot sauce of choice
1 teaspoon pico de gallo powder
⅛ teaspoon fresh ground black pepper
⅛ teaspoon salt

Combine all ingredients in a container of choice. It may be enjoyed immediately but it is more flavorful when set in the fridge to infuse together for at least a couple of hours or overnight. Store, refrigerated, for 2 weeks.

[Traditional Sangrita]

Traditional sangrita uses a sour orange base, which is hard to come by here in the States. To come close to the flavor and make it easy, we are going to use a higher lime juice ratio to add acidity and a sour flavor profile.

1 ounce fresh orange juice

¾ to 1 ounce fresh lime juice (depending on the sweetness of your oranges)

½ ounce Homemade Grenadine (see page 24)

Pinch sea salt

¼ teaspoon chile powder of choice (I use cayenne pepper)

Combine all ingredients in a container of choice. Shake to incorporate. Serve cold. Store in the refrigerator for up to 1 week.

White Peach–Serrano Margarita

I could fill a book with margarita variations but some of the best ones deserve recognition where they can get them. The great thing about this recipe is the control you have over the heat. It's all about control.

1½ ounces reposado tequila
¾ to 1 ounce White Peach Purée (see below)
½ ounce fresh lime juice
½ ounce fresh lemon juice
¾ to 1 ounce Agave Simple Syrup (see page 23)
¼ teaspoon Serrano Tincture, or to taste (see below)

Combine all ingredients in a mixing glass, add ice, and shake hard to fully incorporate the peach purée. Pour into a cocktail glass of choice.

Garnish Idea: Rim of minced serranos mixed with kosher salt (Use a towel to pat the salt mixture dry if having problems with it sticking to the glass.)

[White Peach Purée]

4 whole white peaches

Pit peaches and coarsely chop. Place in a blender or food processor and blend until completely puréed. Add water 1 tablespoon at a time if needed. Strain through a coarse strainer.

[Serrano Tincture]

This technique could be used with any chile, not just serranos. Serranos have more heat than jalapeños, so make sure you are familiar with how much heat you can handle.

1 cup spirit of choice (I use 100% agave reposado tequila)
½ cup finely diced whole chiles (seeds, stems, and all)

Combine ingredients and let sit in a covered glass container (like a Mason jar) for a minimum of 4 hours. The longer, the hotter; I let mine sit overnight. Use your personal taste; 48 hours will give you a nice concentrated heat. However long you let it sit, finish by straining out the chiles and pouring the tincture into a container of choice. Store for a very long time at room temperature. Use the tincture to add heat to everything from hot sauces to, cocktails, and even in cooking.

PEACH

This member of the cherry family is a good source of potassium, minerals, and vitamins A and C. The peach's real value is in the soft fuzzy skin, so make sure you use as much of the peach as you can. Peach works incredibly well with aged spirits, particularly bourbon. This is an incredibly versatile fruit that can be used in almost any form.

Silk Road

Port is a Portuguese fortified wine that comes in many styles. Tawny port specifically is aged in barrels and slowly oxidized. Its nutty flavor profile holds well during reduction and works great with bourbon.

1½ ounces rye or bourbon (I use Wild Turkey)
½ ounce peach liqueur
¼ ounce Tawny Port Reduction (see below)
3 dashes peach bitters

Combine all ingredients in a mixing glass, add ice, and stir until extremely cold. Strain into cocktail glass of choice.

Garnish Idea: Brandied cherry

[Tawny Port Reduction]

3 cups tawny port

Pour the port into a pot and bring to a very light boil over medium-high heat. Reduce by half, 15 to 20 minutes. Remove from heat and store, refrigerated, in a container of choice for up to 1 month.

Peach Caipifruta

Peaches work great with white spirits as well. Try cachaça, which is a Brazilian spirit distilled from sugar cane juice. Not to be confused with rum, cachaça is classified as its own spirit.

¼ ripe peach, quartered
½ lime, skinned
8 ripe blueberries
5 to 6 mint leaves
1 tablespoon superfine sugar
2 ounces cachaça (I use Novo Fogo)

Muddle everything except cachaça in the bottom of a mixing glass, then add cachaça. Add ice and stir to incorporate and chill. Pour into glass of choice.

Garnish Ideas: Fruit and mint, big thick straws to suck up the fruit chunks

Persian Apple

Peach and bourbon is one the strongest chances you'll have to turn a bourbon skeptic into a bourbon lover. The ginger gives this light, fun drink a little zip.

½ yellow peach, chopped
2 ginger slices (quarter-sized)
1½ ounces bourbon
½ ounce amaro nonino
2 dashes peach bitters (orange also works well)
Sparkling wine, to top

Muddle the peach and ginger in the bottom of a mixing glass. Add remaining ingredients except sparkling wine. Shake hard with ice to incorporate the peach flavor, and double strain into a cocktail glass. Top with sparkling wine.

Garnish Ideas: Peach slice, ginger slice

Peachy Keen

Peaches are great blended. The purée has a great mouthfeel and you retain that unique peach flavor. Peaches and cream is a classic combo, and the whipped cream topper makes this a fun, possibly messy, hot weather drink.

2 ounces Black Pepper–Infused Rum (see below)
1 ounce orange liqueur
½ ounce fresh lemon juice
½ ounce fresh lime juice
2 teaspoons brown sugar
1 cup frozen yellow peach slices, about 13 to 15 slices (fresh is preferred; freeze the night before)
½ cup ice

Combine all ingredients in a blender or food processor and blend until peaches are puréed. Pour into glass of choice.

Garnish Idea: Fresh Whipped Cream (see page 81)

[Black Pepper–Infused Rum]

2 cups white rum
1 cup whole black peppercorns

Combine ingredients and let sit in a sealed container for 48 hours, shaking once or twice a day. Strain into container of choice and store for 6 months.

[Fresh Whipped Cream]

1 cup heavy whipping cream

Make fresh cream using a hand mixer or whipping canister. If using a whipping canister, charge with two N_2O cartridges. Refrigerate for 1 hour and shake before using. If using a hand or electric mixer, mix at a medium speed until the cream forms soft peaks. For more flavor, try adding a flavor extract of choice. You can also sweeten the cream by adding powdered sugar or a little agave nectar.

TOMATO

Legally the tomato is a vegetable according to U.S. tariff laws, and considered such in almost every commercial kitchen (even though scientifically it is a berry). The one tomato-based drink that trumps them all is the ever-evolving Bloody Mary. Tomato juice is commonly used in beer as well to make what is called a "red beer." Tomato has a great flavor; try to use fresh tomato juice when possible. It juices very easily in a juicer or with cheesecloth.

Bloody Mary

The Bloody Mary has been through a turbulent history. The recipe demands that people experiment with it. I've even seen recipes with duck fat and bacon grease. This is a simple, straightforward recipe to hit the general palate and a great starting point for creating your own "house" mix.

2 ounces spirit of choice (vodka is traditional)
Homemade Mary Mix, to fill (see below)

Pour spirit of choice into a salt-rimmed Collins glass filled with ice. Fill with the Homemade Mary Mix and stir to incorporate.

Garnish Ideas: Marinated Asparagus (page 27), beef jerky, bacon

[Homemade Mary Mix]

As with Sangrita (page 68), this makes a good marinade.

2 quarts tomato juice (preferably fresh but canned works fine)
¾ cup fresh lemon juice
1 heaping tablespoon prepared horseradish
1½ teaspoons celery salt
1 teaspoon fresh ground black pepper
3 ounces Worcestershire sauce
4 ounces hot sauce of choice
⅛ teaspoon cayenne pepper

Combine all ingredients in a food-safe container and stir. It is preferable to let the mixture sit for 24 to 48 hours to infuse the flavors together, but it can be used right away if desired. Will last up to 7 days, refrigerated.

Baby Steps

This drink is very basic and is for those of you who are scared of drinking something with tomatoes in it. The high-acid tomato goes great with a high-acid wine. This mellow wine-based drink has a mild tomato flavor to it but it barely hangs out in the background. The basil adds its flavor because, let's be honest, there are not too many combinations of flavors that go together as well as basil and tomato.

1 medium-sized basil leaf
½ medium-sized vine-ripened tomato, cut into quarters
6 ounces Riesling or Gewürztraminer

Gently muddle the basil in the bottom of a mixing glass to bruise and release oils. Add the tomato and gently muddle to release just a little bit of juice. Add the wine and ice; stir until frost appears on the outside of the mixing glass (in other words, until very cold). Double strain into a small wine glass.

Garnish Idea: Basil leaf

Americanized Michelada

The Michelada has recently thrust itself onto cocktail menus all over the country. Now a somewhat common blind call, a good Michelada is light and spicy, perfect for those afternoon moments of weakness and commonly consumed to help cure a hangover. If you are not interested in making the Sangrita, you can use plain tomato juice if desired.

Salt-and-Pepper Rim (see below)
2 ounces Americanized Sangrita (see page 68)
½ ounce fresh lime juice
Hefty pinch sea salt
1 dash hot sauce of choice
Light Mexican beer of choice, to fill (I like Victoria)

Rim a pilsner or beer glass with the salt-and-pepper mixture. Fill with ice and add Sangrita, lime juice, salt, and hot sauce. Fill with beer and stir well to incorporate.

Garnish Idea: Salt-and-Pepper Rim (see below)

[Salt-and-Pepper Rim]

¼ cup kosher salt
1 teaspoon fresh ground black pepper
1 lime wedge

Combine salt and pepper together on a plate. Use the lime wedge to moisten the glass, then press glass into mixture.

Urban Farmer

Herbs like thyme are used in cooking with tomatoes all over the world. The herbal flavor of thyme is infused into gin here, which mixes very well with fresh tomatoes.

1 large basil leaf
Pinch dried oregano (optional)
½ Roma tomato, quartered
1½ ounces Thyme-Infused Gin (see below)
¾ ounce fresh lemon juice
¾ ounce Simple Syrup (see page 23)
Soda water, to top

Muddle the basil, oregano, and tomato together in the bottom of a mixing glass. Add the gin, lemon juice, and simple syrup. Shake lightly with ice just to incorporate. Top with soda water as desired.

Garnish Ideas: Slapped basil leaf, thin tomato slice

[Thyme-Infused Gin]

10 sprigs thyme
1 cup gin

Heat a small sauté pan over medium heat. Once hot, add the thyme, and toss for just a minute to bring out the flavors. Transfer to a Mason jar and add the gin. Shake hard and let sit for 8 to 24 hours (taste often to get the flavor you are looking for). I like the vegetal flavor of thyme, so I let this sit overnight.

Nightshade

Even though there is a fennel section, I can't pass up the opportunity to use fresh fennel with tomato. Its sweet, mellow anise flavor always puts a smile on my face. Try a batch of this fennel simple syrup, and you and your partner will be smiling too.

4 honeydew or cantaloupe chunks (grape-sized)
1½ ounces Dried Tomato–Infused Rum (see below)
½ ounce Fennel Seed Simple Syrup (see page 93)
¾ ounce fresh lemon juice
Sparkling water, to top

Muddle the melon in the bottom of a mixing glass. Add remaining ingredients except sparkling water, and shake hard with ice to incorporate. Double strain into a highball glass filled with ice, and top with a splash of sparkling water as desired.

Garnish Ideas: Cantaloupe balls, melon slices, lemon wedge

[Dried Tomato–Infused Rum]

4 vine-ripened tomatoes
2 cups white rum

Cut out the cores of the tomatoes and cut into slices. Place slices into a dehydrator for about a day. They will be still a little soft but it'll be obvious when they are dried. Combine in a container with the rum, shake, and let sit for 7 days. Strain out the tomato slices and store in a container of choice. The flavor will hold for about 1 month, refrigerated. Side note: This infused rum is amazing in a salad dressing or in many cooking applications; experiment!

[Fennel Seed Simple Syrup]

¼ cup whole fennel seeds
1 cup water
1 cup sugar

In a small sauce pan over medium heat, toss in the fennel seeds and stir around until fragrant, just a minute or two. Do not burn. Add the water and sugar and bring to a boil. Strain out fennel seeds after 20 minutes and store syrup, refrigerated, for up to 1 month.

LAVENDER

Lavender can be used in almost every way except for juicing, which may be possible but isn't practical. Infusing is common, as the perfumey flavor is quickly extracted. Lemon juice is a pinnacle flavor complement to lavender and is used in all of the following lavender drink recipes.

Kelli Adams

Soju is a lower-proof spirit distilled from rice. The flavor of rice comes through strongly in this drink, lending a familiar sake flavor profile while holding lavender's hand in a tight squeeze. This drink is a balanced and uniquely flavored gem that will demand to be made twice, or more.

2 ounces Soju or other rice-based distillate
1 ounce fresh lemon juice
1 ounce Lavender Simple Syrup (see below)
1 egg white (optional, but please try it)

Combine all ingredients in a mixing glass and fill with ice. Shake incredibly hard to emulsify the egg white. Strain or double strain into a cocktail glass.

Garnish Idea: Edible flower

[Lavender Simple Syrup]

1 cup water
1 cup sugar
½ cup dried lavender flowers

Heat the water in a saucepan over medium-high heat and add the sugar. Stir until clear. Remove from heat and add the lavender. Stir to wet all the lavender and let sit for 10 minutes. Strain and store, refrigerated, for up to 1 week before it starts to lose its flavor.

Mile High Club

This is based on a classic cocktail from the early 1900s called "The Aviation." The lavender-infused gin plays with the violette liqueur to make this a blast of perfume and nuttiness on your palate.

1½ ounces Lavender-Infused Gin (see below)
½ ounce maraschino liqueur
½ ounce fresh lemon juice
¼ ounce crème de violette

Combine all ingredients in a mixing glass and add ice. Shake and strain into a cocktail glass.

Garnish Idea: Lemon twist

[Lavender-Infused Gin]

⅔ cup dried lavender flowers
1½ cups gin (I use Aviation)

Combine ingredients, stir, and let sit for 4 to 5 hours. Strain and keep in a bottle of choice for months.

Cumber-Some

Cucumber and lavender may seem like an unusual combo at first but once they hook up, infuse their flavors with each other a little, and get pumped up with some citrus and alcohol, they are ready to show you some unique, very nice flavors.

2 cucumber slices (poker chip–sized)
2 ounces cucumber vodka (I use Square One Cucumber)
1 ounce Lavender Honey (see below)
½ ounce fresh lime juice
½ ounce fresh lemon juice
Soda water, to taste

Muddle the cucumber slices in the bottom of a mixing glass. Add remaining ingredients except soda water and shake lightly with ice, just to incorporate. Pour into a Collins glass and top with soda water to taste.

Garnish Idea: Floating thin cucumber slices

[Lavender Honey]

¼ cup honey
½ cup water
¼ cup dried lavender flowers

Combine the honey and water in a pot over medium-high heat until honey dissolves. Stir in the lavender. Remove from heat and let sit for 20 minutes. Strain out lavender, squeezing out as much honey water from the lavender as possible. Store in a squeezable container for up to 2 weeks.

WINE

Learn your wines and drink them often. Wine is a pleasure that has been enjoyed by all the world for thousands of years.

Wanganui Girl

I always equate kiwi with warm weather. The refreshing fruit is very popular around the globe. White wine also makes me think of warm weather, so they got thrown together in a drink. The vodka is present purely to bump up the alcohol content.

1 whole fresh kiwi, skinned
3 ounces Pinot Grigio
½ ounce vodka (I use Skyy)
¾ ounce Simple Syrup (see page 23)

Muddle the kiwi in the bottom of a mixing glass until mushy. Add remaining ingredients and ice. Shake hard to break apart kiwi and strain, if desired, into a cocktail glass or highball with new ice.

Garnish Idea: Kiwi slice

Offering for Kali

Sparkling wine is a perfect blank alcoholic palette for flavors. Hibiscus is a flower with an amazing sour/sweet flavor. The syrup is easy to make and the drink goes down even easier.

1 ounce Hibiscus Syrup (see below)
Sparkling wine, to fill

Pour the Hibiscus Syrup into a champagne glass or coupe. Slowly add sparkling wine, gently stirring to avoid agitating the sparkling wine too much.

Garnish Idea: Dried hibiscus flower

[Hibiscus Syrup]

1 cup water
½ cup sugar
½ cup dried hibiscus flowers

Combine the water and sugar in a pot over medium heat. Once the sugar has dissolved, add the hibiscus flowers and remove from heat. Let sit for 1 hour. Strain and store in a container of choice. Refrigerate for up to 1 week.

Tastes Better in Bed

The Manhattan is one of the greatest cocktails of our time. It is timeless and so simple, yet so hard to make correctly. We are leaning on the typical Manhattan formula here but making a wine syrup in place of the vermouth. Use a good bourbon and enjoy this tossed Manhattan variation.

1½ ounces bourbon (I use Wild Turkey)
¾ ounce Lime Leaf–Wine Syrup (see below)
½ ounce Simple Syrup (see page 23)
¼ ounce orange cordial
2 dashes chocolate bitters

Combine all ingredients in a mixing glass, and add ice. Stir until very, very cold. Strain into a cocktail glass.

[Lime Leaf–Wine Syrup]

2 cups red wine (I use a Bordeaux like Cabernet Sauvignon or Merlot)
½ ounce (loose ½ cup) lime leaves, washed and hand slapped

Combine ingredients in a pot over medium-high heat. Bring to and maintain a very light boil. Reduce mixture by half, 8 to 10 minutes. Strain and store for about 2 weeks, refrigerated.

Bastardo

If you want a fun challenge, pick four ingredients and make them work, somehow.

1 ounce reposado tequila (I use Espolon)
¾ ounce fresh lemon juice
1 ounce Red Wine Syrup (see below)
1 ounce Cocchi Americano

Combine all ingredients in a mixing glass with ice and shake hard. Strain or double strain into a cocktail glass.

Garnish Ideas: Cherry, lemon zest

[Red Wine Syrup]

1 cup red wine (I use a cheap Tempranillo)
1 cup sugar

Combine ingredients in a pot over medium heat until sugar dissolves. Do not bring to a boil. Strain into a container of choice and store for up to 2 weeks.

BIADENE
1.120

Champagne

Champagne. The word itself elicits visions of high profile parties and expensive, large dark bottles being popped open with that very distinct cork-popping sound. Champagne has marketed itself as the end-all in sparkling wine, and even though there are amazingly high-quality sparkling wines, the history and methods of old champagne traditions are a big reason champagne is and always will be so sought after.

Champagne has been used to toast everything from, well, everything. Its aphrodisiac nature is widely known. Imagine finishing a light dinner with your partner and pouring two glasses of champagne to celebrate your relationship. The bubbles go down easy, and soon it's on to glass two. The slightly dry and complex taste is appreciated while you stare for a minute at the mesmerizing bubbles traveling up the glass. Yes, champagne is sexy, there is little doubt.

Buying champagne

There are lots of sparkling wines. You may have heard of Cava or Spumanti, but a bottle can only be called champagne if it is from the Champagne region of France.

Some champagne terms to look for when buying:

Blanc de Noir translates to "white of blacks" and is literally a white wine produced from black or red grapes. Blanc de Blanc translates to "white of whites" and means the champagne is made only from chardonnay grapes.

Rose champagne is a term to describe either the skins of black or red grapes being left in the pressed juice for a certain amount of time or that the pinkish color is obtained by adding a small amount of red wine.

Depending on your palate you may like your champagne drier or sweeter:

* Ultra Brut/Extra Brut/Brut Zero/Brut Nature/Brut Sauvage—*No added sugar*
* Brut—*Nearly dry, contains no more than 1.5% sugar*
* Extra Dry/Extra Sec—*Slightly sweeter, can contain up to 2% sugar*
* Dry/Sec—*Can contain up to 4% sugar*
* Demi-Sec—*Can contain up to 8% sugar*
* Doux—*Sweet, can contain up to 10% sugar*

Champagne has a long and incredibly interesting history. Do a little research and buy your champagne at a wine shop, preferably with a sommelier who knows which direction to steer you in. A note on budget: Good champagne is usually not cheap. Expect to pay $50 and up.

Serving

Please serve champagne cold, 45°F to 48°F. There are store-bought champagne buckets you can fill with ice, but even a large bowl works fine.

Safety

It might seem sexy to launch a cork across the room as your bottle spills all over the place, but it's not practical and can be dangerous. There are many serious accidents that happen every year due to not treating a pressurized bottle with care. When opening a cork, keep your thumb on top of the cork and metal. Unscrew the metal twist slowly, and while keeping your thumb over the cork the entire time, slowly twist with an upward motion and remove. There should only be a hiss or light pop if done correctly.

DAMIANA

Damiana has an interesting history; the shrub is native to both North and South America. The sweet herbal leaves are most common behind the bar in the form of Damiana Liqueur, and have long been used in teas. Its distinct flavor can be played up into something refreshingly herbal and citrusy, or you can leverage its sweetness into a darker, velvety nightcap.

Tramposo

Why try to jazz it up? Damiana, gin, fresh juices, and nothing else makes this drink herbal, fresh tasting, and refreshing.

1½ ounces gin
1 ounce Damiana Liqueur
1 ounce fresh honey tangerine juice (or regular tangerine)
1 ounce fresh grapefruit juice

Combine all ingredients in a mixing glass, add ice, and shake. Strain or double strain into a double old-fashioned glass filled with ice.

Garnish Ideas: Grapefruit wedge or wheel

Don't Fence Me In

Vermouth is easy to make and I'm very surprised that custom vermouths are not utilized more often behind bars. It's as simple as wine, spices, and a fortifier. Your imagination is the limit here.

2 ounces anejo tequila
1 ounce Damiana Vermouth (see below)
1 dash orange bitters
1 dash Angostura bitters

Combine all ingredients in a mixing glass, add ice, and stir until frost forms on the side of the glass. Strain into a cocktail glass.

Garnish Ideas: Brandied cherries, wide peel orange zest

[Damiana Vermouth]

Try the recipe but use as a base for experimentation; there are no rules with homemade vermouth.

1 (750-milliliter) bottle Lillet Blanc or similar aperitif wine
1 heaping tablespoon dried damiana
2 tablespoons Sugar in the Raw
Zest of ½ lemon
Zest of ½ orange
Zest of ½ lime
½ teaspoon whole coriander
10 whole allspice berries
10 whole black peppercornss
5 whole cloves

½ vanilla bean pod, cut open (use pod and seeds)
¼ teaspoon angelica root
⅛ teaspoon ground cinnamon
⅛ teaspoon dried lavender flowers
⅛ teaspoon ground cinchona bark
2 ounces reposado or anejo tequila

Combine all ingredients except the tequila in a pot over medium-low heat and slowly bring to a simmer. Simmer for 20 minutes, then remove from heat. Let sit for an hour to infuse everything together. Strain through cheesecloth into a container of choice. Add tequila and use day of or refrigerate overnight. Will hold flavor for about 1 month, refrigerated.

Hot Dame

Damiana is commonly and traditionally made into a tea. This drink uses the hot toddy formula, so you know it's relaxing and comforting. Snuggle up to someone you like and share this warm and herbal drink.

1½ ounces aged cachaça (I use Novo Fogo)
1 tablespoon agave nectar
Pinch ground cinnamon
Pinch ground allspice
5 ounces boiling hot Damiana Tea (see below)

Combine all ingredients except the tea in a snifter glass, then add hot tea. If making a large batch, you could build in a pot and keep over medium heat, covered. Serve with a ladle into snifter glasses.

Garnish Ideas: Lemon zest, cinnamon stick

[Damiana Tea]

2 heaping tablespoons dried damiana tea
2 cups boiling water

Combine ingredients and let steep for 4 minutes. Strain and use or drink immediately.

POMEGRANATE

Pomegranates are not the only aphrodisiac to originate in the area now known as Iran. It is a common argument that the forbidden fruit was a pomegranate, not an apple. Pomegranates are blessed with such a unique package that their uses are only limited by your imagination. Garnish options using the seeds and skin easily create a sexy look. We are seeing high-quality pomegranate juices and purées on the market in recent years, helping to make pomegranates more popular.

Granada Royale

A couple of drinks in this book are so easy that it's laughable. That's okay because sometimes you don't have all the patience it takes to make a complex multi-ingredient drink. The Granada Royale is very visually appealing with the use of the unique and playfully sexy pomegranate seeds.

Champagne or sparkling wine, to fill
Handful of pomegranate seeds

Fill a champagne glass with champagne or sparkling wine until almost full. Add seeds as desired, squeezing one or two to release some juice.

Beet Your Feet!

Pomegranate and beet are both very unique flavors. You would think that they would clash with each other but they don't fight a bit; they come together and embrace beautifully.

1¼ ounces Roasted Beet–Infused Vodka (see below)
1½ ounces fresh pomegranate juice (or store-bought 100% juice)
½ ounce fresh lemon juice
½ ounce fresh lime juice
¾ ounce Agave Simple Syrup (see page 23)

Combine all ingredients in a mixing glass and add ice. Shake hard and strain into a Collins glass with crushed ice.

Garnish Idea: Thin lemon wheel float

[Roasted Beet–Infused Vodka]

4 large beets
1 (750-milliliter) bottle grain vodka

Wrap beets in tinfoil and roast in the oven for 2 hours at 375°F. Take out and let cool. Skin and slice very, very thinly. Place into a food-safe container and add the vodka. Let sit in the refrigerator for 3 days. Strain and store for a very long time, refrigerated.

Heavy Petting

I love it when a flavor combination comes together in a way that makes you stop what you're doing and just smile. This is easily one of those drinks that demands to be enjoyed on a wooden dock on a warm spring evening—with your partner of course!

2 ounces vodka
1 ounce fresh lemon juice
1 ounce Black Pepper–Ginger Syrup (see below)
Pomegranate soda (I use IZZE), to top

Combine all ingredients except the soda in a mixing glass and add ice. Shake and strain into a Collins glass and top with pomegranate soda to taste.

Garnish Ideas: Lemon wedge, ginger slice, crushed black pepper

[Black Pepper–Ginger Syrup]

1 cup water
1 cup sugar
½ cup minced fresh ginger
2 teaspoons whole black peppercorns

Combine all ingredients in a pot over medium heat. Once sugar is dissolved, turn down to low and cover. Let sit for 30 minutes, then strain into a container of choice.

Spreading the Word

Jams and jellies have become a little more popular behind the bar. In addition to being used as sweeteners, they also give the drink a nice mouthfeel. Some jams and jellies have multiple flavor profiles, which can add complexity. In this case we just want the pomegranate flavor, and the sugar cane–based cachaça is an amazing match.

2 ounces white cachaça (I use Novo Fogo)
1 heaping tablespoon pomegranate jam
½ ounce fresh lime juice
½ ounce Simple Syrup (see page 23)
1 tablespoon egg white

Combine all ingredients in a mixing glass and add ice. Shake extremely hard to emulsify the egg white. Strain into a cocktail glass.

Garnish Ideas: Pomegranate seeds, lime twist

MUSTARD

"Mustard!!!!!! No way in hell am I drinking mustard!" says a guest at my bar as I'm explaining the ingredients in the drink I'm about to put in front of her. It's hard to think about a common condiment, like mustard, being such a delicious and useful ingredient. There must be thousands of different kinds of mustard, and it's easy to make your own. Mustard adds a nice mouthfeel and most importantly, a little zing. Mustard cocktails are not new: a handful of bars around the country list mustard as an ingredient on their menus. All the recipes in this section call for higher-quality mustards, which tend to be pretty light and spicy.

All About Thyming

Mustard goes great with fresh herbs in cooking or in cocktails. Try this drink, which leans on the mojito formula, to see how approachable mustard can be.

- 3 cucumber slices (poker chip–sized)
- 4 fresh tarragon leaves
- 1 (4-inch) sprig fresh thyme
- 2 ounces white rum
- 1 ounce fresh lime juice
- ¾ ounce Raw Sugar Simple Syrup (see page 23)
- ½ to 1 teaspoon coarse Dijon mustard

Muddle the cucumber, tarragon, and thyme lightly in the bottom of a mixing glass. Add the remaining ingredients and ice. Give this a very light couple of shakes, just to incorporate the ingredients, not destroy them. Pour into a tall Collins glass.

Garnish Ideas: Thyme sprigs, tarragon leaves, cucumber spear or wheels

Eye of the Beholder

Fresh apple juice is a weakness of mine! I love the flavor and try my hardest to fit it in when I can—into recipes that is.

2 ounces fresh apple juice
1½ ounces applejack
¼ ounce fresh lemon juice
¼ ounce Homemade Grenadine (see page 24)
¼ ounce Mustard Tincture (see below)

Combine all ingredients in a mixing glass and add ice. Shake hard and double strain into a cocktail glass or highball with crushed ice.

Garnish Ideas: Apple slice, apple zest, lemon wedge

[Mustard Tincture]

1 cup high-proof vodka (I use 160 proof)
1 cup whole yellow mustard seeds

Combine ingredients in a lidded container like a Mason jar and store in a cool, dry place for 2 weeks, shaking once a day to agitate. Strain the mustard seeds out and pour the tincture into a dropper bottle or cleaned-out bitters bottle. Use for up to 1 year.

Planting the Seed

Gin and Campari have been used more times together than I care to imagine, but for good reason. The spicy notes of mustard seed come through on the back end of this fun all-purpose drink.

1½ ounces Mustard Seed–Infused Gin (see below)
¼ to ½ ounce Campari
3 ounces strained pineapple purée
½ ounce fresh lime juice
½ ounce Raw Sugar Simple Syrup (see page 23)

Combine all ingredients in a mixing glass and add ice. Shake hard and strain into a double old-fashioned glass or a cocktail glass with ice.

Garnish Idea: Pineapple slice

[Mustard Seed–Infused Gin]

1 cup whole yellow mustard seeds
1 tablespoon whole black peppercorns
3 cups gin

Combine all ingredients in a lidded jar or container and let sit for 4 to 5 hours, no more, no less. Strain through a coffee filter and store in a sealed jar, refrigerated, for 1 month.

VANILLA

Vanilla isn't going to keep you alive on a desert island with its nutritional content, but it has some very unique properties that benefit any diet.

Compared to other spices, vanilla is one of the most expensive on the planet, second only to saffron. Some of my peers may disagree, but I lean on pure vanilla extracts to get my flavor point across. The reason being, pure (make sure it's pure!) extracts use real vanilla bean with no artificial flavors whatsoever. Be careful still: almost everything we consume that is vanilla flavored is artificial vanillin.

Florentine Codex

Vanilla is a friend with benefits of whiskey because there is usually a touch (or way more) of vanilla flavor in whiskey from the barrel-aging process. This simple to make syrup (and even simpler to make drink) blends well with a strong aged bourbon.

1½ ounces strong overproof bourbon
1 ounce Coffee Bean–Vanilla Syrup (see below)
2 dashes Bittermens Xocolatl Mole Bitters (optional)

Combine all ingredients in a mixing glass and add ice. Stir until extremely cold and strain into a double old-fashioned glass with as large an ice cube as you can fit into the glass.

Garnish Idea: Coffee beans

[Coffee Bean Vanilla Syrup]

1 cup water
½ cup sugar
¼ cup coarsely ground dark roast coffee beans (pulse briefly in blender or coffee grinder)
2 tablespoons pure vanilla extract

Bring the water and sugar to a boil in a medium pot, stirring constantly. Add the coffee and vanilla extract. Remove from heat and let sit for about 2 minutes. Finely strain into container of choice and store for 1 month, refrigerated.

Honeydew List

With the vanilla syrup in this drink, we are using an extract. Using real vanilla beans can take a week or more to infuse, and if you use a pure vanilla extract, which is made from real vanilla beans, you are still drinking a quality product. Just make sure it says pure vanilla on the bottle and has no artificial flavors added.

2 ounces white rum
1 ounce Vanilla Syrup (see below)
1 ounce Honeydew Juice (see below)
½ ounce fresh lemon juice

Combine all ingredients in a mixing glass, add ice, and shake hard. Strain into a Collins glass with new ice.

Garnish Ideas: Honeydew melon slice, melon ball, vanilla bean

[Vanilla Syrup]

1 cup water
1 cup sugar
2 teaspoons pure vanilla extract

In a pot over medium-high heat, bring the water and sugar to a boil and stir until the sugar dissolves. Remove from heat, add the vanilla extract, and pour into a sealable container of choice. Refrigerate for up to 1 month.

[Honeydew Juice]

1 honeydew melon

Scoop out the seeds, skin, and chop the melon. Purée the melon using a food processor or immersion blender in a bowl. Strain through cheesecloth or a strainer and keep for about 1 week, refrigerated.

Wicker Park

There are a number of good vanilla liqueurs on the market. Try one that uses real vanilla bean as part of its flavor profile. If your palate tends to lean on the sweet side, then adjust the amount of vanilla cognac to suit you.

1½ ounces rhum agricole
1 ounce vanilla brandy or cognac (like Navan or Meukow)
1 dash orange bitters
1 dash aromatic bitters
2 drops lavender bitters (I use Scrappy's)

Combine all ingredients in a mixing glass and add ice. Stir until extremely cold. Strain into a cocktail glass.

Garnish Idea: Large orange zest using a Y-peeler

GINGER

Ginger is used in abundance in almost every kitchen and bar; indeed, it's been a staple since the early days of recipe printing. The first documented use was ginger ale, in the classic cocktail The Buck. Ginger beer, which is essentially a much stronger ginger ale, is pinnacle in the Corn 'n' Oil and the famous Moscow Mule. If you've never had either, saddle up at your favorite bar in town or give the Ginger Vodka in this section a whirl.

Ginger Vodka

There is store-bought ginger vodka available but like most things, it's much better if you make it at home. Use a garlic press or food processor to destroy the fibrous ginger and quicken the infusion time. Try it on the rocks with lemon zest or experiment with your own ginger cocktails. If enjoying Ginger Vodka neat, try adding a little simple syrup (see page 23) a teaspoon at a time.

1 pound ginger, peeled and coarsely chopped
Zest of 1 lemon
Zest of 1 lime
2 teaspoons whole allspice berries
1 (750-milliliter) bottle grain vodka

Take the chopped ginger and press as much of it as you can with a garlic press (or mince instead), dumping everything into a large Mason jar or other sealable container. Add the lemon zest, lime zest, and allspice. Pour in the vodka and set in a cool, dark area where you will shake it once or twice a day. Infuse for at least 7 days (or longer if desired). After infusion, finely strain, squeezing out all the liquid from the ginger, into a bottle of choice.

Ginger-Caramel Margarita

Caramel and ginger might seem like an unusual combination at first. But if you can imagine a caramelly flavor with the first sip that starts to turn spicy and complex as it finishes into citrusy strong goodness, you will realize instantly that ginger and caramel are made for each other.

1 teaspoon diced ginger
1½ ounces reposado tequila
1 ounce Caramel Syrup (see below)
½ ounce fresh lime juice
½ ounce fresh lemon juice

Muddle the ginger in the bottom of a mixing glass until an almost mushy substance is made. Add remaining ingredients and shake hard with ice to incorporate flavors. Pour into a double old-fashioned glass.

Garnish Ideas: Candied ginger, lime wheel

[Caramel Syrup]

¾ cup caramel syrup (I use Monin)
¼ cup hot water

Mix ingredients together until a uniform liquid forms. Store for 1 month, refrigerated.

Sexauer's Ginger Beer

Although it is non-alcoholic, many a drink recipe calls for ginger beer and house made, as usual, is best. Powdered dried gingerroot is typically used as a flavoring for recipes such as gingerbread and cookies but lacks the nutritional benefits and full flavor of the fresh stuff. I like to use a combo of both to achieve as complex a ginger flavor as I can.

1 recipe Liquid Ginger Sauce (see below)
2 ounces fresh lemon juice, finely strained
2 ounces fresh lime juice, finely strained
6 ounces Simple Syrup (see page 23)
10 ounces cold water

Combine all ingredients in a soda siphon canister. Screw on lid and charge with a CO_2 cartridge. Refrigerate for 1 to 2 hours and use as desired. Makes 1 quart (size of most iSi soda siphons).

Garnish Ideas: Lemon wheels or wedges

[Liquid Ginger Sauce]

1 cup minced fresh ginger
1½ cups water
¼ teaspoon ground ginger
⅛ teaspoon sea salt
5 whole allspice berries
3 whole cloves

Bring all ingredients to a boil in a medium saucepan over medium-high heat, then reduce to a simmer over medium-low heat and cook for 1 hour, covered. Let cool and strain through cheesecloth until all liquid is extracted. You should have approximately 1½ cups of liquid.

Zut Alors

This drink is a tricky one. Gastriques are a powerful tool once mastered. The sweet, acidic flavoring of the vinegar is key to balancing the cognac and ginger liqueur.

1¼ ounces VS Cognac (brandy will work equally well)
¾ ounce ginger liqueur (I use Domaine de Canton)
¾ to 1 ounce Green Apple Gastrique (see below)
⅓ ounce fresh lemon juice
¼ ounce dry vermouth

Combine all ingredients in a mixing glass, add ice, and shake hard to incorporate the flavors. Strain or double strain into a cocktail glass of choice.

Garnish Idea: Thin green apple slice

[Green Apple Gastrique]

1 tablespoon fresh lemon juice
½ cup sugar
¼ cup water
½ cup apple cider vinegar
2 tablespoons whole coriander seeds
¼ teaspoon whole allspice berries
1 cup fresh green apple juice (I use an electric juicer)

In a medium saucepan over high heat, combine the lemon juice, sugar, and water. Continue to cook using a pastry brush or spatula to stir the sugar mixture. When the mixture turns a light brown, slowly stir in the vinegar. Once mixed, add the coriander seeds and allspice. Allow to reduce slightly for about 2 minutes. Add the apple juice and continue stirring. Remove from heat and allow the mixture to cool. Strain out spices and pour into a sealable bottle of choice. Makes enough for about 12 drinks. Keeps for about 2 weeks, refrigerated.

FIG

Figs are not so easy to work with in cocktails. When was the last time you saw a fig drink on a cocktail menu? There are precious few. The trick with figs is to find ways to make sure the flavor is not lost, especially when up against a big aged bourbon or brandy. The sweet flavor of figs work well with the vanilla and spice profiles of most aged spirits.

Framboise Me

Raspberry framboise is perfect on its own for those romantic nights. Now double it up with an aphrodisiac like fig and you've got a drink that hits the right spot every time.

1½ ounces vodka (I use Skyy)
1 tablespoon fig jam
1 teaspoon fresh lemon juice
1 ounce raspberry framboise
1 to 1½ ounces chilled soda water (optional)

Combine all ingredients except soda water in a mixing glass and add ice. Shake hard to incorporate flavors and double strain into a large champagne glass. Top with cold soda water to taste, which helps lighten this somewhat heavy drink.

Garnish Ideas: Lemon twist, lemon zest, raspberries

Sleaze Noir

The deep, strong flavors of fig work nicely with a little citrus, and hold the hand of rum very well.

1½ ounces black strap/seal rum
1½ ounces Fig Purée (see below)
½ ounce fresh orange juice
½ ounce fresh lime juice
½ ounce Honey Simple Syrup (see page 23)

Combine all ingredients in a mixing glass and shake very hard with ice to incorporate the flavors. Double strain into a double old-fashioned glass over new ice.

Garnish Ideas: Orange zest, half or whole fig

[Fig Purée]

2 cups water
15 dried figs, quartered (try Kalamata or Calimyrna)

Bring ingredients to a boil in a saucepan over high heat. Cover and simmer on low heat for 15 minutes. Remove from heat and let cool (still covered) for 10 minutes. Pour figs and liquid into a blender or food processor and purée until smooth, adding additional water if needed 1 tablespoon at a time to get a thick but pourable purée. Pour into a container of choice and keep for up to 1 week in the refrigerator.

Mission Do-Able

This fig concoction is for the whiskey lover. Rye tends to have a spicy note that works well with the flavor of the fig, and a slight anise on the back end. This big bad sipper might be gone sooner than you think, so savor the moment.

2 ounces Mission Fig–Star Anise–Infused Rye (see below)
½ ounce fresh tangerine juice
½ ounce fresh lemon juice
½ ounce Agave Simple Syrup (see page 23), optional
½ ounce averna

Combine all ingredients in a mixing glass, shake with ice, and strain or double strain into a cocktail glass.

Garnish Idea: Star anise float

[Mission Fig–Star Anise–Infused Rye]

1 whole star anise
7 ounces dried black mission figs, quartered
1 (750-milliliter) bottle rye or bourbon (I use Wild Turkey)

Combine all ingredients in a Mason jar and put in a cool, dark place. Shake at least once a day to agitate. After 7 days, finely strain and store in a bottle of choice for up to 3 months.

ROSEMARY

Rosemary is best used sparingly. Even just stirring it into a cocktail will impart its unique aromatics into the mix. Rosemary is suited perfectly for garnishing, as it looks the part but also can be functional because of the intense smell. Roasting is almost a must for utilizing its amazing aroma.

Dripping Dew

This is essentially a cosmopolitan recipe using the Rosemary-Infused Cherry Juice in place of the cranberry juice. I've never been a huge fan of store-bought sweetened cranberry juice (which is usually only about 20% juice), so this is a nice deviation.

2 ounces vodka (I use Skyy)
1 ounce Rosemary-Infused Cherry Juice (see below)
½ ounce fresh lemon juice
½ ounce fresh lime juice
¼ to ½ ounce Agave Simple Syrup (see page 23)

Combine all ingredients in a mixing glass, add ice, and shake. Strain into a cocktail glass of choice.

Garnish Idea: Small rosemary sprig

[Rosemary-Infused Cherry Juice]

6 rosemary sprigs (6 to 8 inches)
4 cups 100% cherry juice

Toss and stir the rosemary in a pan over medium-high heat until an intense aroma comes out, only a minute or two. Do not burn. Combine rosemary and cherry juice together in a sealable container and refrigerate for 24 to 48 hours. Strain out the rosemary and store juice in a container of choice for up to 1 week in the refrigerator.

Fertile Garden

Bell pepper juice is a fun ingredient to work with. It has a very unique flavor quality that works wonderfully with the herbaceousness of gin and rosemary.

⅓ yellow bell pepper, washed and seeded
1½ ounces gin (I use Aviation)
½ ounce fresh lemon juice
¾ ounce Rosemary Simple Syrup (see below)

Muddle the bell pepper in the bottom of a mixing glass until it is almost a mushy purée. Add the remaining ingredients and shake hard with ice to extract the pepper flavor profile. Pour into a double old-fashioned glass.

Garnish Ideas: Large bell pepper slice, candied bell pepper, large rosemary sprig

[Rosemary Simple Syrup]

5 sprigs rosemary (6 to 8 inches)
1 cup water
1 cup sugar

Remove the rosemary leaves from the stems, discard stems, and put the leaves in a pan over high heat (smell fingers and smile). Toss and stir the rosemary until it becomes a little dry and extremely fragrant, 3 to 5 minutes. A handful of the leaves may turn brown; it's fine. Add the water and sugar to the pan and stir until the sugar is dissolved. Remove from heat and let cool, at least 10 minutes. Strain out the rosemary and refrigerate.

Women of Anthos

Verjus is an incredible sweet/sour/acidic lemon juice or vinegar substitute. Pisco is the national spirit of Peru and is distilled from grapes. This is a refreshingly light, slightly low-alcohol cocktail that demands to be inside of you quickly.

6 watermelon chunks (grape-sized)
1 teaspoon sugar
1 ounce Rosemary-Infused Pisco (see below)
1¼ ounces white verjus

Muddle the watermelon chunks and sugar in the bottom of a mixing glass. Add the remaining ingredients and shake hard with ice. Double strain into a cocktail glass.

Garnish Ideas: Watermelon slice, watermelon ball, rosemary sprig

[Rosemary-Infused Pisco]

10 to 12 sprigs rosemary (6 to 8 inches)
1 (750-milliliter) bottle unaged Peruvian pisco

Remove the rosemary leaves from the stems, discard stems, and put the leaves in a pan over high heat. Toss and stir the rosemary until it becomes a little dry and extremely fragrant, 3 to 5 minutes. A handful of the leaves may turn brown; it's fine. Combine the roasted rosemary in a jar with the pisco. After 4 hours, strain out the rosemary and pour infused pisco into a container of choice.

HONEY

Honey is everywhere and commonly used in cocktails. More so recently, as people are reading about its healthy qualities, especially compared to processed sugar. The flavor profile of honey works perfectly with fall and winter drinks. Bourbon is a favorite base spirit with honey but anything and everything works.

Cot in the Act

Bourbon and apricot can be bullies a lot of the time with their strong flavor profiles. Only honey has the tone and weight to bring them down to earth. The apricot flavor is bumped up using both a good store-bought apricot liqueur and a housemade apricot syrup.

2 ounces bourbon
½ ounce apricot liqueur (I use Luxardo)
½ ounces Apricot-Honey Syrup (see below)
½ ounce Cocchi Americano
1 dash Angostura bitters

Combine all ingredients in a mixing glass and stir with ice. Strain into a cocktail glass of choice.

Garnish Ideas: Dried apricot, lemon wheel, lemon twist

[Apricot-Honey Syrup]

1 cup lightly packed dried apricots, quartered
¼ cup honey
1 cup water

Combine all ingredients in a pot over medium-high and bring to a boil. Stir, cover, and reduce heat to simmer for about 15 minutes. Remove from heat and let cool for another 15 minutes. Strain out apricots, pressing out as much juice as possible, and store in a container of choice for up to 2 weeks, refrigerated.

I Mead You

Mead is a wine made from honey. There are entire books dedicated to mead; just use one that is semi-sweet. The vodka is present only to bump up the alcohol, not take away from the mead's flavor; adjust as desired. This drink is served hot, so it is really enjoyed late at night or when the weather is so cold you need someone close to keep you warm.

2 ounces mead
½ ounce vodka
1 teaspoon honey
2 ounces Chamomile Tea, boiling (see below)
1 large cinnamon stick
Pinch ground nutmeg
2 whole cloves

Combine all ingredients in a pot over medium-low heat, keep covered, and heat until hot, about 15 minutes. Using a ladle, pour into a snifter or mug that has been rinsed with boiling (or really hot) water, and serve.

Garnish Ideas: Cinnamon stick, floating whole cloves

[Chamomile Tea]

8 ounces boiling water
2 tablespoons dried chamomile flowers (or 4 tea bags)

Combine ingredients, let sit for at least 5 minutes, then strain and serve.

Juniper's Girl

The mint, sage, and gin combine together in way that works in harmony with the raspberry and honey. The honey adds a dynamic that only honey can add.

4 good-sized raspberries
2 large sage leaves
6 large mint leaves
2 ounces gin
1½ ounces Honey Simple Syrup (see page 23)
½ ounce fresh orange juice
½ ounce fresh lime juice

Muddle the raspberries, sage, and mint together in a mixing glass with ice. Add remaining ingredients and shake with ice. Double strain into a cocktail glass.

Garnish Idea: Sage leaf

CARDAMOM

Cardamom ranks as the world's third most expensive spice. It is in the same family as ginger; and like ginger is regarded as an aphrodisiac. Most of the benefits of cardamom are woven into folklore and Arabic medicinal practices. There are many studies showcasing cardamom as a beneficial spice, most notably as an aid to digestion. Tummy soothing aside, cardamom's complexity and unique flavor profile are virtues behind the bar.

Linear Thinking

Cardamom bitters are a great way to express the flavor of cardamom into a cocktail. You can easily find them online, or search for a homemade recipe if you really feel like a challenge.

1½ ounces bourbon
¾ ounce Drambuie
½ ounce sweet vermouth
¼ ounce Bénédictine
1 dash cardamom bitters (I use Scrappy's)

Combine all ingredients in a mixing glass and stir with ice. Strain into a cocktail glass.

Garnish Ideas: Brandied cherry, thin lemon wheel

Embracing Njallani

Aquavit is a caraway- and anise-forward spirit. Caraway and cardamom complement each other well. Rhubarb is a great flavor that holds the hands of both these spices.

2 whole cardamom seeds
1½ ounces aquavit (I use Krogstad)
¾ ounces Rhubarb Syrup (see below)
¾ ounce fresh lemon juice

Muddle the cardamom in the bottom of a mixing glass. Add remaining ingredients and shake hard with ice to infuse the cardamom flavor. Double strain into a double old-fashioned glass filled with new ice.

Garnish Idea: Lemon twist

[Rhubarb Syrup]

1 cup water
1 cup sugar
3 stalks rhubarb, rinsed and cut into 1-inch pieces

Combine all ingredients in a pot over medium-high heat and bring to a boil. Lower heat to medium-low and simmer for 20 minutes. Remove from heat and let cool. Strain through cheesecloth, squeezing out the rhubarb juice into a container of choice. Keep, refrigerated, for up to 2 weeks.

Voyage

IPA is an extremely hoppy beer in the pale ale family. Using beer in cocktails is pretty common, and you can see them peppered into menus across the country. We are reducing the beer in this recipe to really bring out a unique flavor that works with cardamom.

1 whole cardamom seed
1½ ounces bourbon
1 ounce IPA Syrup (see below)
½ ounce averna

Muddle cardamom in the bottom of a mixing glass. Add the remaining ingredients and shake hard with ice to extract the cardamom flavor. Double strain into a cocktail glass.

Garnish Ideas: Orange zest, orange slice or half wheel

[IPA Syrup]

24 ounces IPA (2 bottles of beer)
½ cup sugar

Pour the beer into a pot over medium-high heat. Bring to a light boil, stirring frequently, and reduce by half. Remove from heat, add the sugar, and stir until it's completely dissolved.

BANANA

Using bananas in cocktails is, well, interesting. Bananas don't juice and are typically used in a smoothie style of drink. Banana daiquiri anyone? I always lean toward using fresh ingredients instead of sugary and artificially sweet liqueurs. These banana-flavored cocktail recipes all use fresh bananas in one way or another.

Bend of the Bract

Banana and tequila are pretty good friends. The end result is a thick, viscous drink that demands a very fat straw to suck down.

- ½ medium-sized ripe banana
- 1½ ounces 100% agave reposado tequila (I use Espolon)
- 1 ounce Honey Simple Syrup (see page 23)
- ½ ounce fresh lime juice
- ½ ounce fresh lemon juice

Muddle the banana in the bottom of a mixing glass until mushy. Add remaining ingredients and ice. Shake extremely hard to break up the banana. Pour into a Collins glass of choice.

Garnish Ideas: Banana slice, lemon wedge, lime wedge

Carver's Nightcap

Peanut butter might not be the first thing on your mind when you think of cocktails, but don't pass up this drink because of the unknown. It's hard to put down, and to top it off, you have an interesting problem of having extra peanut butter. . . .

2 ounces bourbon

1 tablespoon creamy peanut butter

1½ ounces Banana Simple Syrup (see below)

½ ounce fresh lemon juice

Combine all ingredients in a mixing glass and add ice. Shake hard to incorporate the peanut butter. Pour into an old-fashioned glass.

Garnish Ideas: Banana slice, dab of peanut butter on top

[Banana Simple Syrup]

1 cup water

1 cup sugar

1 banana, diced

Combine the water and sugar in a medium pot over medium heat. Once all the sugar has dissolved, remove from heat. Put the diced banana into a bowl and pour the hot syrup over the top. Cover and refrigerate for a minimum of 4 hours or overnight. Strain out the banana chunks and pour the syrup into a container of choice. Store, refrigerated, for up to 2 weeks.

Tai Me Up

This recipe is based on the Mai Tai but replaces the orgeat syrup with banana liqueur, which helps the other flavors work together instead of fighting for attention.

1 ounce white rum
1 ounce aged rum
1 ounces Banana Liqueur (see below)
¾ ounce fresh lime juice
1 dash Angostura bitters
1 dash orange bitters

Combine all ingredients in a mixing glass, add ice, and shake. Strain or double strain into a cocktail glass.

Garnish Ideas: Lime wedge, caramelized lime wedge, floating thin banana slice, thin floating lime wheel

[Banana Liqueur]

½ cup water
½ cup sugar
1 recipe Roasted Banana Purée (see page 199)
1 cup white rum

Combine the water and sugar in a pot over medium-high heat. Stir until sugar is dissolved and liquid is clear. Add the banana purée, remove from heat, and let cool. Add the rum and pour contents into a sealable container. Keep refrigerated and shake once a day for 3 days. Coarsely strain out most of the banana then finely strain using a clean french press or cheesecloth. Store, refrigerated, for up to 1 month.

[Roasted Banana Purée]

2 large bananas, unpeeled

To ensure maximum banana flavor, we are going to roast them. Adjust oven rack to upper-middle position and preheat oven to 325°F. Place bananas on baking sheet and bake until skins are completely black, about 15 minutes. Let cool 5 minutes. Scoop the banana flesh into a food processor and purée. Makes about 1 cup.

The Double Mahoi

Bananas are rightfully doomed to be blended. Since they don't juice well, a banana shake can be a mouthwatering drink. This recipe uses milk instead of cream to lighten it so you can have two or three without filling up.

- 2 ounces dark rum
- 1 cup whole milk
- 1 banana, cut into chunks
- 1 tablespoon sugar
- ¼ teaspoon ground cloves
- ⅛ teaspoon pure vanilla extract
- 2 cups ice

Combine all ingredients in a blender. Blend until smooth and pour into a tall Collins glass.

Garnish Idea: Sprinkle powdered cloves on top

FENNEL

An ingredient used in absinthe, fennel has a taste similar to anise and licorice. The seeds have been thought to improve everything from breath to strength and have long been associated with boosting a woman's libido.

Fennel and fennel seed are a surprising glue to thousands of food and drink recipes. The seeds have a slight licorice flavor, though not as overpowering. The seeds are commonly infused into simple syrups or alcohol, which are usually the best vehicles for their flavor.

Double Fenneled

Fennel is great with citrus. The soft, sweet anise flavor keeps this drink interesting from start to finish.

1 pineapple chunk (prune-sized)
1½ ounces Roasted Fennel Seed Vodka (see below)
¼ ounce Simple Syrup (see page 23)
1 ounce fresh orange juice
½ ounce fresh lemon juice
½ ounce Ramazzotti

Muddle the pineapple in the bottom of a mixing glass. Add remaining ingredients, shake hard with ice, and strain over new ice into a double old-fashioned glass.

Garnish Ideas : Orange slice, pineapple slice or chunk

[Roasted Fennel Seed Vodka]

½ cup fennel seeds
1 cup vodka

Place a pan over medium-high heat. Once the pan is hot, add the fennel seeds. Toss for no more than a minute. A crackle or two is normal. You just want to enhance the flavor of the fennel, not burn or cook it. Combine fennel seeds with vodka and let sit for 4 hours, then strain into container of choice.

Stealing Fire

Fennel lends its subtle anise flavor to this intense and complex herbal cocktail. Sip slowly and enjoy the flavors as they change from initial taste to back end flavor.

1 teaspoon Roasted Fennel Seeds (see below)
1¼ ounce reposado tequila (I use Espolon)
½ ounce yellow Chartreuse
½ ounce fresh yellow grapefruit juice
½ ounce orange liqueur
2 dashes grapefruit bitters

Muddle the fennel seeds in the bottom of a mixing glass. Add remaining ingredients and shake hard with ice. Double strain into a cocktail glass.

Garnish Ideas: Fennel leaf sprig, grapefruit zest

[Roasted Fennel Seeds]

1 teaspoon fennel seeds

Place a pan over medium-high heat. Once the pan is hot, add the fennel seeds and toss for no more than a minute. A crackle or two is normal. You just want to enhance the flavor of the fennel, not burn or cook it.

The Gala

Fresh apple juice and whiskey do well to have a third flavor join in. Fennel is able to enter the mix and spice things up, but just a little. Fennel knows that too much of its unique flavor will compete instead of complement. A fresh-tasting fall sipper, this drink is a great way to see how fennel mixes with alcohol.

1½ ounces bourbon
1 ounce fresh apple juice (try Gala apples)
½ ounce Raw Sugar–Fennel Syrup (see below)
½ ounce fresh lemon juice
Sparkling wine, to top

Combine all ingredients, except sparkling wine, and shake with ice. Double strain into a cocktail glass then top with sparkling wine.

Garnish Ideas: Gala apple zest or slice

[Raw Sugar–Fennel Syrup]

2 tablespoons whole fennel seeds
1 cup water
1 cup Sugar in the Raw

Place a pan over medium-high heat. Once the pan is hot, add the fennel seeds. Toss for no more than a minute. A crackle or two is normal. You just want to enhance the flavor of the fennel, not burn or cook it. Add the water and sugar, stir until sugar dissolves. Remove from heat and let sit, covered, for 30 minutes. Strain and store in a container of choice for up to 1 month.

CINNAMON

Cinnamon is commonly used in almost every bar, for everything from topping and rimming to syrups and infusions. Let's face it, cinnamon sticks are just plain sexy.

A Nudge and a Wink

Blueberries have a lot of pectin in them, which lends a nice mouthfeel to this drink. The lemon juice helps lighten it up a bit and the lemon thyme infusion adds a great complexity to this delicious cinnamon-touched cocktail.

15 fresh blueberries
2 ounces Lemon Thyme–Cinnamon–Infused Vodka (see below)
½ ounce fresh lemon juice
¼ to ½ ounce Simple Syrup (see page 23)

Muddle the blueberries in the bottom of a mixing glass. Combine remaining ingredients and add ice. Shake extremely hard and double strain into a cocktail glass or double old-fashioned glass with new ice.

Garnish Ideas: Blueberries, lemon twist

[Lemon Thyme–Cinnamon–Infused Vodka]

10 long sprigs lemon thyme
1 cinnamon stick (about 4 inches long)
2 cups grain vodka

Place a pan over medium-high heat. Once the pan is hot, add the thyme and cinnamon. Stir and toss continuously for only a minute or so to help release flavor. Remove from heat and combine with the vodka in a sealable jar. Let sit at room temperature for 24 hours. Strain and store in a container of choice for up to 3 months.

Sexauer's Spiced Wine

This spiced wine will fill your house for the rest of the night with a scent reminiscent of the holidays, baked cookies, and fresh coffee cake. Do not boil the wine, it will oxidize! Taste often, especially if you are deviating from the recipe. The longer the spices sit, the stronger they will infuse into your wine, which can be good or bad depending on the spice. Be especially careful with cloves, as they are very potent. When serving, I find using a soup warmer, crock pot, or even a cleaned-out coffee pot works well to keep the wine warm throughout the night.

1 (750-milliliter) bottle Syrah (I use a big Syrah with notes of plum)
3 small cinnamon sticks
4 whole cloves
8 whole peppercorns
8 whole allspice berries
1 cup brown sugar
¼ cup brandy
Zest and juice of 1 orange
Zest and juice of 1 lemon
1 tablespoons pure vanilla extract
1 tablespoon honey

Pour the entire bottle of wine in a large pot with a lid. Grind or pound cinnamon, cloves, peppercorns, and allspice, then add to the wine. Add the remaining ingredients to the wine, cover, and heat on low for 30 minutes. Remove from heat and let cool for 10 minutes to finish infusing spices into the wine. Strain and pour wine into a sealable container. It is much better to refrigerate overnight if you have the time to let the flavors infuse more, but either way be sure to reheat and serve warm (it's not so good cold).

Spice it Up

Cinnamon is a great spice to work with but there's a balance. It can overpower easily. The homemade cinnamon syrup is not too sweet and uses Vietnamese (Saigon) cinnamon. Not your grocery store cinnamon, it has an intense spicy flavor to it. Look for it online or at a local spice shop.

1½ ounces brandy
1 ounce fresh orange juice
1 ounce Saigon Cinnamon Syrup (see below)
¼ ounce aperol
¼ ounce sweet vermouth
1 dash Fee Brothers Old Fashion Aromatic Bitters

Combine all ingredients in a mixing glass, add ice, and shake hard. Strain into a cocktail glass.

Garnish Ideas: Pinch of cinnamon, orange slice

[Saigon Cinnamon Syrup]

1 cup water
¼ cup sugar
1 tablespoon ground Vietnamese cinnamon

Combine all ingredients in a pot over medium heat and stir until well mixed, and sugar is dissolved. Finely strain to remove the ground cinnamon.

CHOCOLATE

The fact that chocolate is an aphrodisiac is known by almost everyone . . . but why? Like all the aphrodisiacs in this book, there is no concrete evidence to prove that chocolate stimulates sexual feeling, but when used in the right circumstances it certainly adds to the mood.

Chocolate liqueurs are readily available and easy to make at home, where you can supervise the sugar content. The sweetness of chocolate may confine it to dessert drinks mostly, but it's not the rule.

Chupas Mi Champurrado

This is a very traditional Mexican drink and as far as I know, not typically added to alcohol. This chocolate-based drink has been part of Mexican culture for centuries using the same base as tortillas to thicken it. Something about the mouthfeel of this makes it incredibly appealing. As it cools this may get so thick that you'll need a spoon to finish it!

1½ ounces anejo tequila
5 ounces Champurrado (see below)

Pour the tequila into a snifter glass or mug and add the Champurrado. Stir and serve.

Garnish Ideas: Chocolate chunks or shavings

[Champurrado]

1½ cups warm water
½ cup masa (corn tortilla flour)
2½ cups whole milk
1 cup condensed milk
½ cup chopped chocolate
½ cup light brown sugar
¼ teaspoon ground anise seeds
¼ teaspoon ground cinnamon

Put the warm water in a large saucepan over medium heat, and slowly whisk in the masa until incorporated. Stir in the remaining ingredients, whisking occasionally for about 15 minutes. Bring mixture to a boil and remove from heat, stirring constantly for a couple minutes. Use immediately.

Chocolate Manhattan

The Manhattan is arguably one of the world's greatest and most popular cocktails. The simple recipe below leaves the Manhattan intact and shows how powerful and useful bitters can be. Don't be scared of bitters; remember, it's okay to try everything once. I'm using bourbon because the sweeter butterscotchy flavor works perfectly with the chocolate bitters. Look for them online if you can't find them locally.

2 ounces overproof bourbon
1 ounce (or to taste) sweet vermouth
3 to 4 dashes chocolate bitters (I use Scrappy's)

Combine all ingredients in a mixing glass, add ice, and stir until the mixing glass is coated with frost and condensation, and the drink is cold as can be. Strain into a cocktail glass.

Garnish Idea: Chocolate shavings

The White Orange

The chocolate martini is old and dated. Try this orange and white chocolate cocktail at home to see how using the right ingredients can make all the difference in the world.

2 ounces White Chocolate Liqueur (see below)
¼ ounce vodka (I use Skyy)
¼ ounce orange liqueur
2 dashes orange bitters
1 dash chocolate bitters (optional)

Combine all ingredients in a mixing glass and add ice. Stir until very cold and strain into a cocktail glass or double old-fashioned glass with new ice.

Garnish Ideas: Orange slice, orange zest, dark chocolate shavings

[White Chocolate Liqueur]

2 cups water
1 cup white chocolate chips
1 cup sugar
1 cup grain vodka

Combine all ingredients except vodka in a pot over medium heat, stirring frequently, until chocolate is melted. Remove from heat and add vodka. Pour into a sealable container and refrigerate overnight to infuse the flavors. Shake extremely well before using, as solids will form. Will keep for about 2 weeks, refrigerated.

Mayan Hot Chocolate

There are two hot chocolate drinks in this section because the relaxing and lulling effect of chocolate served hot is too much to pass up. Mayan hot chocolate has roots going back to the very beginnings of Mayan culture, and the heat of the jalapeño with the chocolate creates an ever so slight burn on your lips, tongue, and throat.

1 to 2 thin jalapeño slices (optional if you can't take the heat)
1½ ounces pisco
6 ounces Hot Chocolate (see below)

Muddle the jalapeño in the bottom of a mixing glass, add pisco, and fill with Hot Chocolate. Stir quickly and strain into a hot mug or glass.

Garnish Ideas: Whipped cream, foamed milk

[Hot Chocolate]

3 cups milk
½ cup half-and-half
⅓ cup water
⅓ cup minced chocolate of choice
¼ cup sugar
¼ teaspoon pure vanilla extract
Pinch salt

Combine all ingredients in a pot and heat over medium-high heat until hot, fully melted, and mixed. Use immediately.

NUTMEG

Nutmeg is usually used freshly ground, as a garnish. Please don't stop at garnishes, though; give it a try in infusions and syrups. The smell of cooked nutmeg filling the house is a must.

A Warm Night in Banda

Nutmeg infuses well—almost too well; keep tasting the infusion to make sure the flavor doesn't get too intense. Disclaimer: Consuming large quantities of nutmeg can have unwanted side effects. This is due to myristicin, a compound within nutmeg that can be toxic in high doses. Out of common sense, limit the consumption of this cocktail to two per night.

1 ounce Nutmeg-Infused Dark Rum (see below)
1 ounce aged rum
½ ounce House Falernum (see below)
½ ounce aromatic bitters (I use Angostura)
¼ ounce fresh lime juice

Combine all ingredients in a mixing glass. Add ice and shake hard. Strain into a cocktail glass.

Garnish Ideas: Lime or orange zest, grated nutmeg

[Nutmeg-Infused Dark Rum]

4 whole nutmeg pods, gently cracked open
2 cups dark rum

Combine ingredients in a sealable container and let sit for 4 days, shaking occasionally. Strain into a container of choice and keep for up to 1 month.

[House Falernum]

1 tablespoon whole cloves
1 tablespoon whole allspice berries
1 cup water
1½ cups sugar

2 tablespoons fresh ginger, minced
4 limes, finely zested
¼ teaspoon almond extract
3 ounces fresh lime juice
1½ cups white rum

In a hot pan over medium-high heat, toss the cloves and allspice, only for a minute to release flavor. Add the water, sugar, and ginger. Bring to a boil, then remove from heat. Let cool for about 15 minutes and then add the lime zest, almond extract, lime juice, and rum. Pour into a clean Mason jar and refrigerate for at least 8 hours. Strain through a cheesecloth and squeeze out all the liquid. Store in a container of choice for up to 2 weeks, refrigerated.

Rompope

Rom-what? Rompope, pronounced "rum-pope-a" is easily described as Mexican eggnog. Using milk in place of cream or half-and-half lightens this up enough that you can enjoy two or three without filling up as much as you would with overly sweet store-bought eggnog. Side note: You can substitute the brandy out for pretty much anything. A hit of smoky mezcal gives this drink a little depth.

1 egg
3 ounces whole milk
¾ ounce Agave Simple Syrup (see page 23)
1½ ounces brandy
¼ ounce smoky mezcal (optional)
1 dash vanilla extract
1 dash almond extract
Pinch ground cinnamon
Pinch ground nutmeg

Combine all ingredients in a shaker and shake very, very hard with ice to emulsify the egg. Strain into a glass of choice (double old-fashioned and small wine glasses work well).

Garnish Idea: Ground nutmeg

Tight Squeeze

Jicama has a unique flavor with a slight sweetness to it. Pick jicamas that are small to medium sized, not the overly huge ones (they have more starches and less flavor). This cocktail is a great way to see tequila shine outside of the margarita formula.

1½ ounces reposado tequila (I use Espolon)
¾ ounce Jicama Syrup (see below)
¾ ounce cream sherry

Combine all ingredients in a mixing glass and add ice. Shake and strain into a cocktail glass.

Garnish Ideas: Ground nutmeg, lime zest

[Jicama Syrup]

1 cup water
1 cup sugar
1 cup diced jicama
2 tablespoons fresh ground nutmeg

Combine all ingredients in a pot over medium-high heat and stir until sugar is dissolved and mixture comes to a boil. The nutmeg will not dissolve. Remove from heat and let sit to cool for at least 15 minutes to infuse flavor. Strain through a very fine strainer or cheesecloth to remove most of the nutmeg. Store in a container of choice for up to 2 weeks.

OTHER SIPS

caviar

Some aphrodisiacs just don't need an entire section. Lots of people think of oysters and being turned on, but I'm not about to fill an entire section with oyster drinks. The remaining recipes are strictly for fun and inspiration. Sometimes an aphrodisiac is so ingrained in history it demands to be written about, whether it's meant to be drunk or not. At the very least, have a sense of humor about the next round of recipes; they're designed with adventure in mind. Remember, I always treat a recipe as a foundation, not gospel. Finally, consuming cocktails should be about having fun, which isn't talked about enough. Enjoy yourself trying some of the following off-the-wall recipes.

Secret Rendition

Pine nuts are often used in cooking. They have a unique flavor that complements most Asian cuisine especially well.

1½ ounces pisco
½ ounce orange liqueur
¼ ounce fresh key lime juice (regular limes will work if needed)
1 ounce Pine Nut Milk (see below)
1 dash Angostura bitters

Combine all ingredients in a mixing glass. Add ice and shake hard. Strain into a cocktail glass.

Garnish Idea: Thin key lime wheels

[Pine Nut Milk]

2 cups pine nuts
3½ cups water
1 cup sugar
1 ounce vodka
¼ teaspoon orange blossom water, or to taste

Roast the pine nuts in a large oven-safe pan at 400°F for no more than 10 minutes, tossing once or twice. Pulse pine nuts in a food processor just to break up. (Not too much, you don't want pine nut butter; you can even just chop the pine nuts as well. You're looking for pine nut crumbles.) Pour pine nuts back into the hot pan on a stove top over high heat. Add the water and sugar, and bring to a boil. Once boiling, let simmer for 1 hour, then remove from heat and let sit for another 5 to 6 hours. Strain through a cheesecloth or chinoise to remove as much of the "milk" as you possibly can. Add the vodka and orange blossom water and store in a container of choice, refrigerated, for about 1 week.

21st-Century Tea Party

According to a 2002 study, Southern Illinois University School of Medicine found an increased libido in laboratory animals using both the American and Asian forms of ginseng.

Ginseng is hard to come by in the states. A practical way to use it is to find it in tea and infuse the ginseng tea into a spirit. The infusion doesn't take that long, and the flavor can be great depending on the quality of the tea you use. Another note: You can infuse this into any spirit you would like, not just rum.

2 ounces Ginseng Tea Rum (see below)
1 ounce Bärenjäger (or other good honey liqueur)
1 dash Angostura bitters

Combine all ingredients in a mixing glass and add ice. Stir and strain into a cocktail glass.

Garnish Idea: Lemon zest

[Ginseng Tea Rum]

2 cups aged rum
2 tablespoons ginseng tea (or any tea containing ginseng)

Combine ingredients and let sit for 12 to 24 hours; taste often to get the flavor you want. Finely strain and store in a container of choice for up to 3 months.

Roy and Gouda

After all these kitchen ingredients, now we're talking about cheese drinks? Cheese is a dairy product and has hundreds, if not thousands, of flavor profiles. Dairy and distilled spirits have been friends for a long time; think of drinks like the White Russian.

Let's talk about cheese for a minute. Think about the aroma. Many cheeses can resemble the scent of a woman and can be stimulating for both sexes. This delicacy contains phenylethylamine (PEA), which is related to the release of endorphins. PEA is also in cacao, but some cheeses can contain many times the amount as chocolate.

2 ounces scotch
1 ounce sweet vermouth
2 dashes Angostura bitters
Frozen Smoked Gouda Foam (see below), to top

Combine all ingredients except the gouda foam in a mixing glass and add ice. Stir until very cold; you should see frost on the outside of the glass. Strain into a cocktail glass and top with a frozen foam shape.

Garnish Idea: Frozen Smoked Gouda Foam (see below)

[Frozen Smoked Gouda Foam]

2 cups (8 ounces) diced smoked gouda
½ cup whole milk
¼ cup olive oil
1 teaspoon kosher salt
¾ cup heavy cream

Combine all ingredients except the heavy cream in a food processor. Blend until the cheese is puréed, about 2 minutes depending on the machine. Pour and push through a cheesecloth (or preferably a chinoise) into a bowl. Mix in the cream, then pour contents into a 1-pint iSi whipping canister and charge with a N_2O cartridge.

On a baking pan, make stars or shapes with the foam and freeze. It can take as little as 15 minutes to freeze. Once cold, it will hold shape and have a lot less bleeding. As you drink, the cheese will slowly start to thaw and should be the last thing you taste.

Oysters with Cucumber Vodka Jelly

Don't worry, we are not going to turn oysters into cocktails; in fact, we're going to do the opposite. We are turning our cocktail into an oyster topper. To do this we are going to use a little gelatin to get the consistency we want. I like the idea of complementing and enhancing the cucumber flavor of the oyster; essentially we're going to make a fancy Jell-O shot to top our oysters. If you want to enjoy a quivering burst of flavor, this is how to use oysters the aphrodisiac way.

½ cup water
¼ cup raspberry vinegar
5 sheets gelatin
2 cups vodka
½ cup Cucumber Purée (see below)
¼ cup fresh lemon juice
½ cup sugar
12 Kumamoto oysters

Heat the water, vinegar, and gelatin in a pot over medium heat. Once the gelatin is dissolved, add in remaining ingredients except oysters; remove from heat. Pour into a bread pan and refrigerate for at least 6 hours, or until you've got a jelly-like substance.

To serve, shuck an oyster, leaving the oyster in the half shell. Take a square of the jelly and set it on top. Eat the oyster-jelly combo together. Makes enough for at least 3 dozen oysters.

Garnish Idea: Thin cucumber slice

[Cucumber Purée]

2 cups chopped peeled cucumbers
½ cup water

Combine ingredients in a blender and blend until the mixture is a watery purée.

Caviar and Vodka

Caviar and vodka are seen together for many reasons but the main one is flavor. Vodka is flavorless, especially when cold, and caviar is packed full of intense flavor, so the two complement. Putting some caviar at the bottom of a glass and pouring ice cold vodka on top gives you a crisp, clean alcohol flavor at first. As you sip down and get closer to the caviar you start to taste some of those flavors. Then, you take your mother-of-pearl spoon (steel will impart a bad flavor; traditionally and practically, a mother-of-pearl spoon is used to consume caviar) and scoop up the caviar and eat it. The downhill roller coaster of flavor from crisp and strong to intense and unique have been enjoyed for generations.

1 teaspoon caviar (I use paddlefish)
3 ounces vodka (I use Skyy)

Place the caviar in the bottom of a champagne flute or port glass. Vigorously shake the vodka in a mixing glass with ice until very cold. (You can also put the vodka in a freezer and freeze, but that is a matter of personal taste. I like water to mellow out the sometimes intense strength of some vodkas but again, do what you like and do what tastes good.) Pour vodka over caviar.

Garnish Idea: Mother-of-pearl spoon

A note on caviar

Caviar is clearly considered a delicacy in most cultures, and the highbrow price in the United States keeps the generalization going that caviar is only for the rich. Too bad. There are a large number of high-quality caviars using sustainable techniques as to not continue the decline the world's wild sturgeon population. Combine that fact with higher availability (online) and knowing that prices are not as exorbitant as people may think, and you have a new tool for entertaining at home.

Served simply as an hors d'oeuvre or in a unique presentation, caviar is visually appealing and eye-catching. Although some caviar is expensive, try paddlefish. An ounce can go for around $25 and is a great introduction to the flavors and look of caviar.

If you are lucky enough to live in a city with a caviar shop, go there. It will by and large be your best bet for finding what you are looking for and most likely you can taste the product before you buy.

Absinthe

Absinthe is absolutely the most misunderstood spirit in history. I am listing this as an aphrodisiac drink because so many people believe it to be true. The impression of absinthe, that you will hallucinate or black out, is because of many pre-Prohibition conspiracies and old-school politics. It doesn't help that modern marketing has further exaggerated the folklore, combining their products (which are typically nothing like real absinthe) with marketing ploys to make them seem more interesting and sexy.

Today you can purchase absinthe brands that are "real," meaning that they contain the same species of wormwood and are close in flavor profile to pre-ban absinthes. Thujone, the primary volatile oil in wormwood, is present only in trace amounts in absinthe due to its resistance to distillation. You will never "trip," hallucinate, or do anything different than you normally do when you're drinking alcohol.

When enjoying absinthe with your partner, it's entertaining to read some of the old writings about absinthe and its effects. Check out www.wormwoodsociety.org for everything you need to know about absinthe. The Wormwood Society has a web presence but it is also very active in outreach, education, and events. In the meantime, go to the liquor store, carefully pick up a bottle of absinthe (you should never see the word "artificial" on the label), and enjoy it in a very traditional way. Try Marteau, Pacifique, Delaware Phoenix, Ridge Verte, or La Grenouille, to name a few.

Tip:

Don't light a sugar cube on fire or bring fire into the picture. At all. This is not the traditional way of enjoying absinthe and you will only add a burnt flavor profile to the delicate complexities of absinthe.

How to Enjoy Absinthe Properly

Water

Absinthe is in the 106 to 148 proof range, and is not intended to be drunk neat. Water is part of any good absinthe experience.

Spoon

The absinthe spoon is a unique experience embraced by the spirit. The holes in the spoon allow the water to break down the sugar and mix into the glass. A long dinner fork will suffice if you do not feel the need to purchase an absinthe spoon, although many are available online and in specialty shops.

Sugar

The sugar cubes used in the past and in Europe are not the same as our common pressed and perfectly square sugar cubes, but they will work just fine. Some people prefer no sugar, some one cube, and some two or more. It is merely a matter of taste.

The glass

You can find them online of course, but try Goodwill or other secondhand stores. Any glass will work, but there are certain ones more suited. Most bars specializing in absinthe will have a glass with a bubble at the bottom, originally made to help with measuring dilution. I see small wine glasses and champagne glasses used as well. A standard pour at most restaurants and bars tends to be 1½ ounces. An absinthe pour should only be 1 ounce.

The pour

With 1 ounce of absinthe in the glass place the absinthe spoon across the top and set a sugar cube in the middle.

However you pour the water, whether it's a pitcher or absinthe drip, use ice cold water. Pour a small amount of water onto the sugar, saturating it and letting it sit for a minute or two so that the sugar begins to loosen and dissolve. Begin again by slowly dripping or very slowly pouring water onto the sugar cube, filling your glass. Only personal taste and experience will get you to your desired dilution, but a standard starting point is a 3:1 ratio of water to absinthe. Adjust up and down from that and also take into account the proof of your absinthe. Continue pouring water until your ratio is achieved and the sugar cube is dissolved.

When the water-to-absinthe ratio reaches a certain level, the essential oils, which are dissolved in the absinthe during distillation, will emulsify with the water and create an opalescent cloudy effect known as the "louche."

Take your absinthe spoon and give your drink a stir to help with any sugar that is not dissolved.

Sit back and relax. Slowly sip and enjoy your absinthe, taking in the anise, fennel, and herby flavors that so many people enjoy around the world.

fin

Index